Contents

Preface and Acknowledgments

Over the past decade, we have worked with hundreds of teachers and administrators as they implement the SIOP® Model. SIOP (Sheltered Instruction Observation Protocol) comprises eight components: Preparation, Building Background, Comprehensible Input, Strategies, Interaction, Practice and Application, Lesson Delivery, and Review and Assessment. Within the eight components are thirty features of effective sheltered instruction that have been found to improve English learners' academic achievement when they are implemented consistently and systematically (Echevarria, Vogt, & Short, 2004).

This book responds to a frequent request from elementary and secondary teachers for additional ideas and instructional strategies that can be used within the SIOP Model. The activities within this book are grouped within each of the eight SIOP components. The features for the components are listed at the beginning of each section. Each activity includes sample content and language objectives, a must for effective SIOP lessons.

As you thumb through this book, you will recognize some familiar activities. We hope you will also find some new ideas that will make the content you teach more comprehensible for your students, especially those who are learning English. The activities were created and selected based upon the following criteria:

- the degree to which the activities promote students' interactions with each other and with the teacher;

- the opportunities for students to use the English language through reading, writing, listening, and speaking; and

- the ease with which the activities can be implemented for nearly any content or grade level.

The SIOP Model serves as an instructional framework that operationalizes effective sheltered instruction for students acquiring English. The Model incorporates familiar, research-based, and time-honored teaching practices. Therefore, many of the cooperative learning and other activities that you already use are appropriate to use within the SIOP Model. We hope this new collection of ideas and activities that have been recommended by SIOP trained teachers will add to your repertoire and further enhance your instruction and students' learning.

Preface and Acknowledgements

If you're working with teachers or if you're currently teaching yourself, it is important to remember that activities are not the end; rather, they are the means to the end. The end we all aim for, of course, is mastery by all students of content objectives, language objectives, and district/state content standards. While some teachers just want activities for activities' sake, as coaches, supervisors, and fellow teachers, we all have a responsibility to help these teachers learn to use a variety of instructional strategies in a purposeful, thoughtful, and careful manner in order to maximize student achievement.

We have made every attempt to track down the originators of the ideas and activities that are included in this publication. If you know of any that we have not included, please let us know.

Special thanks go to Angie Aldrich Medina, an expert SIOP teacher, who shared many ideas that she and her colleagues have used with their English learners. Finally, we express our thanks to our SIOP colleague, Deborah Short, and to our families who lovingly (and with great patience) support our SIOP work.

—MEV

JE

A Guide to Using This Book

Which of the eight components the activity supports

The name of the activity

How the activity supports the SIOP model

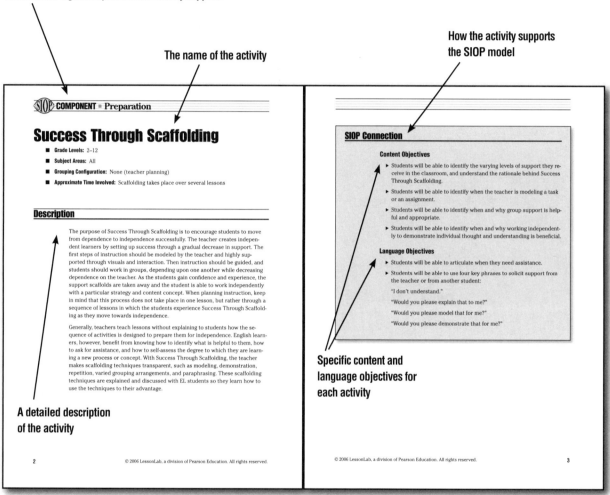

SIOP COMPONENT ▪ Preparation

Success Through Scaffolding

- **Grade Levels:** 2–12
- **Subject Areas:** All
- **Grouping Configuration:** None (teacher planning)
- **Approximate Time Involved:** Scaffolding takes place over several lessons

Description

The purpose of Success Through Scaffolding is to encourage students to move from dependence to independence successfully. The teacher creates independent learners by setting up success through a gradual decrease in support. The first steps of instruction should be modeled by the teacher and highly supported through visuals and interaction. Then instruction should be guided, and students should work in groups, depending upon one another while decreasing dependence on the teacher. As the students gain confidence and experience, the support scaffolds are taken away and the student is able to work independently with a particular strategy and content concept. When planning instruction, keep in mind that this process does not take place in one lesson, but rather through a sequence of lessons in which the students experience Success Through Scaffolding as they move towards independence.

Generally, teachers teach lessons without explaining to students how the sequence of activities is designed to prepare them for independence. English learners, however, benefit from knowing how to identify what is helpful to them, how to ask for assistance, and how to self-assess the degree to which they are learning a new process or concept. With Success Through Scaffolding, the teacher makes scaffolding techniques transparent, such as modeling, demonstration, repetition, varied grouping arrangements, and paraphrasing. These scaffolding techniques are explained and discussed with EL students so they learn how to use the techniques to their advantage.

A detailed description of the activity

SIOP Connection

Content Objectives

▸ Students will be able to identify the varying levels of support they receive in the classroom, and understand the rationale behind Success Through Scaffolding.

▸ Students will be able to identify when the teacher is modeling a task or an assignment.

▸ Students will be able to identify when and why group support is helpful and appropriate.

▸ Students will be able to identify when and why working independently to demonstrate individual thought and understanding is beneficial.

Language Objectives

▸ Students will be able to articulate when they need assistance.

▸ Students will be able to use four key phrases to solicit support from the teacher or from another student:

"I don't understand."

"Would you please explain that to me?"

"Would you please model that for me?"

"Would you please demonstrate that for me?"

Specific content and language objectives for each activity

2

3

▪ SIOP Features ▪

1. Content objectives clearly defined for students

2. Language objectives clearly defined for students

3. Content concepts appropriate for age and educational background level of students

4. Supplemental materials used to a high degree, making the lesson clear and meaningful (e.g., graphs, models, visuals)

5. Adaptation of content (e.g., text, assignment) to all levels of student proficiency

6. Meaningful activities that integrate lesson concepts (e.g., interviews, letter writing, simulations, models) with language practice opportunities for reading, writing, listening, and/or speaking

Success Through Scaffolding

▪ **Grade Levels:** 2–12

▪ **Subject Areas:** All

▪ **Grouping Configuration:** None (teacher planning)

▪ **Approximate Time Involved:** Scaffolding takes place over several lessons

Description

The purpose of Success Through Scaffolding is to encourage students to move from dependence to independence successfully. The teacher creates independent learners by setting up success through a gradual decrease in support. The first steps of instruction should be modeled by the teacher and highly supported through visuals and interaction. Then instruction should be guided, and students should work in groups, depending upon one another while decreasing dependence on the teacher. As the students gain confidence and experience, the support scaffolds are taken away and the student is able to work independently with a particular strategy and content concept. When planning instruction, keep in mind that this process does not take place in one lesson, but rather through a sequence of lessons in which the students experience Success Through Scaffolding as they move towards independence.

Generally, teachers teach lessons without explaining to students how the sequence of activities is designed to prepare them for independence. English learners, however, benefit from knowing how to identify what is helpful to them, how to ask for assistance, and how to self-assess the degree to which they are learning a new process or concept. With Success Through Scaffolding, the teacher makes scaffolding techniques transparent, such as modeling, demonstration, repetition, varied grouping arrangements, and paraphrasing. These scaffolding techniques are explained and discussed with EL students so they learn how to use the techniques to their advantage.

SIOP Connection

Content Objectives

- ▶ Students will be able to identify the varying levels of support they receive in the classroom, and understand the rationale behind Success Through Scaffolding.

- ▶ Students will be able to identify when the teacher is modeling a task or an assignment.

- ▶ Students will be able to identify when and why group support is helpful and appropriate.

- ▶ Students will be able to identify when and why working independently to demonstrate individual thought and understanding is beneficial.

Language Objectives

- ▶ Students will be able to articulate when they need assistance.

- ▶ Students will be able to use four key phrases to solicit support from the teacher or from another student:

"I don't understand."

"Would you please explain that to me?"

"Would you please model that for me?"

"Would you please demonstrate that for me?"

Task Analysis

(or Backward Planning)

- **Grade Levels:** All
- **Subject Areas:** All
- **Grouping Configuration:** None (teacher planning)
- **Approximate Time Involved:** 5–20 minutes (during lesson preparation)

Description

The purpose of Task Analysis (also called Backward Planning) is to ensure that instruction leads to student success on the final assessment of a lesson's content and language objectives. During lesson planning, the teacher determines how the content and language objectives will be assessed. When the assessment is predetermined, a quick pretest can be used to assess prior knowledge about the content concepts. A predetermined assessment keeps the instruction focused on the objectives of the lesson and helps to create an environment for success.

It is also important for teachers to plan backward from the final assessment and think about what students need to know and be able to do in order to be successful on the assessment of content and language objectives. If students are unable to understand or complete a task, the teacher should step back and reteach or explain the concept in a different way before moving on. Too often, teachers do not realize that some students have been lost throughout the lesson until students complete the final assessment. Task Analysis can prevent this from happening.

If the teacher explains how students will be assessed at the beginning of a lesson when content and language objectives are presented, students will better understand how instruction and tasks correlate with the eventual assessment.

Note: *While Task Analysis is important for all grade levels, older students (grade 3–12) will benefit most from a careful explanation of how lessons are planned and taught.*

SIOP Connection

Content Objective

Students will be able to make the connection between the content being taught and the content being assessed. They will know that their assessment has been planned prior to instruction.

Language Objective

Students will be able to ask what will be assessed at the end of a lesson using clarifying language, such as:

"What information will I need to remember?"

"Is that an important part of our assessment?"

"What part of this information is most important?"

The Four Domains of Language

(or Language Processes)

- ■ **Grade Levels:** All
- ■ **Subject Areas:** All
- ■ **Grouping Configuration:** None (teacher planning)
- ■ **Approximate Time Involved:** 5–30 minutes (while preparing lessons)

Description

The Four Domains of Language—reading, writing, listening, and speaking—are essential to learning English. Language objectives should reflect that students will be reading, writing, listening, and speaking throughout lessons. Reading and listening are receptive processes, while speaking and writing are productive (students produce language orally and/or in writing). When learning a new language, the receptive processes (listening and reading) may come more quickly while the productive processes (writing and especially speaking) may come later. However, it is critically important to plan lessons so that ELs can practice all four processes. They must have opportunities to receive and process information, as well as produce language to transmit information to others.

Depending on the English language proficiency levels of the students, some or all of the Domains of Language may need to be supported to promote student success. It is important to keep in mind that language acquisition is a process that is as unique as your students. As the Four Domains of Language are incorporated into lessons, students may feel more successful in some areas than in others. Through repeated practice in all of the domains, students will learn that reading, writing, listening, and speaking are interrelated processes that build upon one another.

If you discuss with students how reading, writing, listening, and speaking are interrelated and why they are important to gaining English language proficiency, you might use the following content and language objectives.

SIOP Connection

Content Objective

Students will be able to explain how using the Four Domains of Language during a lesson will help them master the content objectives at the same time they are learning English.

Language Objective

Students will be able to complete the following sentences:

"Reading helps me learn by _____."

"Writing helps me learn by _____."

"Talking to other people helps me learn by _____."

"Listening to other people helps me learn by _____."

SIOP Flow Chart

(Adapted from Long Beach Unified School District)

- ▪ **Grade Levels:** All
- ▪ **Subject Areas:** All
- ▪ **Grouping Configuration:** None (teacher planning)
- ▪ **Approximate Time Involved:** 30–60 minutes (during unit preparation)

Description

The purpose of the SIOP Flow Chart is to create an overview of an entire unit of lessons. It is used to plan a scope and sequence of both language and content objectives, through 12 (or any number) days of instruction. The SIOP Flow Chart also encourages reading, writing, and discussion (listening and speaking) connections. Teachers who regularly use the SIOP Flow Chart will begin to see how their language and content objectives can be sequenced to build upon one another throughout a unit.

SIOP Connection

This particular Preparation activity does not lend itself to specific content or language objectives. For teachers who are very familiar with the SIOP's eight components and 30 features, the SIOP Flow Chart serves as a guide to lesson and unit planning and development.

See sample SIOP Flow Chart on next page.

Subject:_____   **SIOP Flow Chart**   **Date:**_____

1 | Unit:

Lesson Focus:

Content Objectives:

Language Objectives:

Reading/Writing/Discussion
Activities:

2 | Unit:

Lesson Focus:

Content Objectives:

Language Objectives:

Reading/Writing/Discussion
Activities:

3 | Unit:

Lesson Focus:

Content Objectives:

Language Objectives:

Reading/Writing/Discussion
Activities:

4 | Unit:

Lesson Focus:

Content Objectives:

Language Objectives:

Reading/Writing/Discussion
Activities:

5 | Unit:

Lesson Focus:

Content Objectives:

Language Objectives:

Reading/Writing/Discussion
Activities:

6 | Unit:

Lesson Focus:

Content Objectives:

Language Objectives:

Reading/Writing/Discussion
Activities:

7 | Unit:

Lesson Focus:

Content Objectives:

Language Objectives:

Reading/Writing/Discussion
Activities:

8 | Unit:

Lesson Focus:

Content Objectives:

Language Objectives:

Reading/Writing/Discussion
Activities:

9 | Unit:

Lesson Focus:

Content Objectives:

Language Objectives:

Reading/Writing/Discussion
Activities:

10 | Unit:

Lesson Focus:

Content Objectives:

Language Objectives:

Reading/Writing/Discussion
Activities:

11 | Unit:

Lesson Focus:

Content Objectives:

Language Objectives:

Reading/Writing/Discussion
Activities:

12 | Unit:

Lesson Focus:

Content Objectives:

Language Objectives:

Reading/Writing/Discussion
Activities:

Building Background

▪ SIOP Features ▪

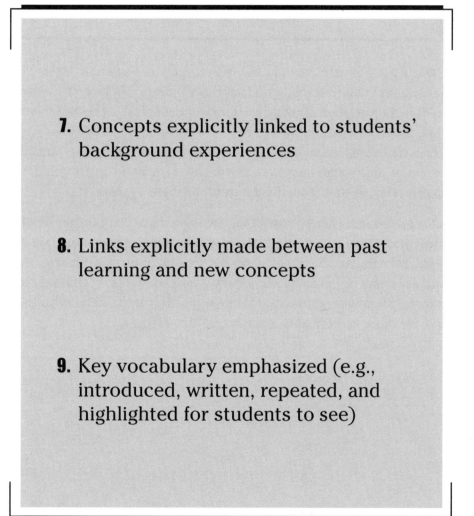

7. Concepts explicitly linked to students' background experiences

8. Links explicitly made between past learning and new concepts

9. Key vocabulary emphasized (e.g., introduced, written, repeated, and highlighted for students to see)

Realia, Photos, and Illustrations

■ **Grade Levels:** All

■ **Subject Areas:** All

■ **Grouping Configurations:** Individual, partners, small groups, whole class

Description

The purpose of using realia (real items, such as a miner's scale, globe, or apple), photos, and illustrations, is so that the students can have a clearer image of an unknown or new vocabulary word or concept. The more hands-on and three-dimensional the realia the better. The teacher can introduce key vocabulary words or the class can generate a list for a particular topic. It is best to keep the lesson or unit vocabulary on a word wall, a chart, or in personal vocabulary dictionaries so that students can refer to them as needed.

After introducing a new vocabulary word with realia, photos, or illustrations, ask students to turn to a partner and in a complete sentence include the vocabulary word, referring to the physical object (realia, photo, or illustration) and word wall (or chart or personal dictionary) as needed. For beginning English speakers, provide them with a sentence frame until they are familiar with the procedure and are more comfortable speaking with a partner.

SIOP Connection

Content Objectives

▶ Students will be able to use vocabulary related to a content concept (such as transportation).

▶ Students will be able to identify realia, photographs, and/or illustrations using the appropriate labels and vocabulary (such as for varied modes of transportation).

Language Objective

Students will be able to use a sentence frame. For example:

"When I go to _____ I travel by _____."

In this example, students will place a vocabulary word in the first blank that is related to different places they go (e.g., *to school, the store, my grandmother's*). In the second blank, students will place vocabulary words that have been introduced for the lesson on transportation (e.g., *car, bike, train, plane, boat, subway, scooter*).

KWL Chart

(From Ogle, 1986)

- **Grade Levels:** All
- **Subject Areas:** All
- **Grouping Configurations:** Individual, partners, small groups, whole class

Description

One of the best ways to activate prior knowledge and build background is the familiar KWL (or KWHL) chart. The purpose of a KWL chart (what we Know, what we Want to learn [or what we Wonder about], and what we have Learned) is to assess students' knowledge about a topic, uncover misconceptions, and (most important) allow students input about what they would like to learn about the topic.

Before brainstorming ideas for each section of the KWL, give students some quiet thinking time (approximately 2–3 minutes). In the first box, record all information the students brainstorm, even if it is inaccurate. (Clarification can take place when the third box is completed after reading, learning about, and discussing the topic.) During the introduction of a lesson or unit, complete the first two sections of the KWL. Use the third box throughout the unit, adding information each day. Clarify misconceptions during discussion. Post the KWL throughout the unit so students can refer back to it as needed.

If desired, insert a box for H for (How we find out). This box can be inserted before the L (what we have Learned) box. In this new box, students generate ideas for sources that can be researched to find additional information about the topic.

SIOP Connection

Content Objectives

- ▶ Students will be able to brainstorm what they already know about (a topic, e.g., animal habitats).

- ▶ Students will identify what they would like to learn about (the topic).

- ▶ Students will be able to list what they have learned about (the topic).

- ▶ Students will be able to confirm or disprove information on the chart, while adding new information that was learned.

Language Objective

Students will be able to use the following sentence frames to state whether information is something they already know, is something they want to learn about, or is something they learned through the course of instruction.

"I Know that _____."

"I Want to know _____."

"I Learned that _____."

Unit or Lesson Topic

What We Know	What We Want to Learn	What We Have Learned

Pretest with a Partner

(Adapted from Angie Medina, Long Beach Unified School District)

- **Grade Levels:** 2–12
- **Subject Areas:** All
- **Grouping Configuration:** Partners

Description

The purpose of Pretest with a Partner is to allow English learners the opportunity to preview at the beginning of the lesson or unit the material that will be assessed at the conclusion of the lesson or unit. The teacher distributes one pretest and one pencil to each set of partners. The pretest should be similar or identical to the posttest that will be administered at the end of the lesson or unit. The students pass the pretest and the pencil back and forth between one another. They read the question aloud, discuss the possible answer, and come to a consensus, and write the answer on the pretest. They continue in this manner until all questions are answered. This activity provides an opportunity for the students to share any background knowledge they may have with a partner, while the teacher circulates around the room to assess students' background knowledge and to note any areas where knowledge is lacking.

SIOP Connection

Content Objectives

▶ Students will be able to preview (the topic content) by taking a pre-test with a partner.

▶ Students will be able to share knowledge while making predictions and asking questions about pretest items of which they are unsure.

Language Objective

Students will be able to use questioning and clarifying terms to help initiate discussion with their pretest partner:

"Do you know anything about that?"

"I'm not sure about the answer, but I do know _____."

"I think the answer might be _____, because I learned _____."

Backwards Book Walk

(Adapted from Bonnie Bishop, Long Beach Unified School District)

- ■ **Grade Levels:** 2–12

- ■ **Subject Areas:** Science, social studies, English language development (ELD)

- ■ **Grouping Configurations:** Individual, partners, small groups, whole class

Description

The purpose of a Backwards Book Walk is to familiarize students with a nonfiction text before they begin to read it independently. The Backwards Book Walk begins with the conclusion, so that students can understand the overall meaning of the text (book or chapter) before looking at the bits and pieces. After the conclusion is read, the students then continue in the backwards manner reading headings, captions, and keywords. This provides an introduction to important vocabulary so that students will better comprehend the text information. Finally, after the entire chapter has been viewed, ask students to guess the title of the text. Give some *quiet* thinking time, and then encourage students to share their thoughts with partners. Afterward the partners can share ideas with the class. This activity reverses the process of the typical picture or text walk, and motivates students through the novelty of something new, while at the same time demonstrating a technique for prereading nonfiction text.

SIOP Connection

Content Objectives

▶ Students will be able to read the conclusion of (a text) and use other textual features to make predictions about what they will learn while reading the text.

▶ Students will be able to add to or change predictions while reading (the text).

Language Objective

Students will be able to use the following sentence frames after doing a backwards walk through (a book or chapter):

"The conclusion and other text features make me think that we are going to learn _____."

"We might learn about _____."

"I don't think this chapter will be about _____."

Go to Your Corner

(Adapted from the Reading and Writing for Critical Thinking [RWCT] Project of the International Reading Association)

■ **Grade Levels:** All

■ **Subject Areas:** All

■ **Grouping Configurations:** Partners, small groups, whole class

Description

The purpose of Go to Your Corner is to give students an opportunity to share their knowledge about a topic. This also allows students to practice their paraphrasing skills. Choose a topic that has at least four possible dimensions. Assign each dimension to a specific corner of the room. This works best if you label the corners and include a picture of the topic. Ask students to move to a particular corner based on interest or to provide each student with a word or picture related to one of the corners. Once students are in their corners, ask them to pair with a partner to explain why they chose that corner. Give pairs ample time to talk. Then ask students from each corner to share their reasons with the class. You may choose to chart their ideas.

Here's an example activity: Give each student an index card with a picture and/or word that describes one of four Native American tribes. Ask students to walk around the room, sharing and then trading their index cards with other students. Call "Freeze!" and then ask students to move to the corner where the tribe on their card is represented. When all students are assembled in one of the four corners, tell students to share their cards with the other students. Ask groups to come to consensus about whether the picture or word is related to their particular tribe. If a student is not in the correct corner, other students can help direct him or her to the appropriate tribe.

This activity has many possibilities. It can be carried into a discussion, writing assignment, or graphic organizer that classifies the information about each dimension of the topic.

SIOP Connection

Content Objective

Students will be able to classify information about four aspects of (a topic, e.g., four Native American tribes) by going to a designated corner.

Language Objective

Students will be able to explain the connection between a picture/word on an index card and the particular topic (e.g., Native American tribe) that it describes, using the following prompts:

"This is a word related to the _____ topic (e.g., tribe) because _____."

"This is a picture related to the _____ topic (e.g., tribe) because _____."

The Insert Method

(Adapted from the Reading and Writing for Critical Thinking [RWCT] Project of the International Reading Association)

- ■ **Grade Levels:** 3–12
- ■ **Subject Areas:** All
- ■ **Group Configurations:** Partners, small groups, whole class

Description

With partners, students read together a nonfiction article. While reading, they insert the following codes directly into the text they are reading:

- A check mark (✔) indicates a concept or fact that is already known by the students.

- A question mark (?) indicates a concept or fact that is confusing or not understood.

- An exclamation mark (!) indicates something that is unusual or surprising.

- A plus sign (+) indicates an idea or concept that is new to the reader.

When the partners finish reading and marking the text, they share their markings with another pair. If any misconceptions or misunderstandings are cleared up, then the question mark is replaced with an asterisk (*). When groups finish working, the whole class discusses text with the teacher.

SIOP Connection

Content Objectives

▶ Students will be able to use a coding system while reading (a nonfiction text) to identify concepts or facts that are familiar, those that are confusing, and those that are new, unusual, or surprising.

▶ Students will be able to clarify misconceptions and misunderstandings about (a text) while working with group members.

Language Objectives

▶ Students will be able to ask questions about concepts and facts that are confusing.

▶ Students will be able to read and discuss (a piece of nonfiction text) about (a topic) with group members.

Student Journals

- ■ **Grade Levels:** 1–12
- ■ **Subject Areas:** All
- ■ **Grouping Configurations:** Individual, partners, small groups, whole class

Description

The purpose of Student Journals is for students to reflect back on their previous learning and have the opportunity to build on that knowledge while reading and writing about a topic. Journals also help the teacher to better understand what the students are learning (or remembering) from the lesson or unit. Student Journal writing (or drawing for very young children and beginning English speakers) can be completed before, during, and/or after a lesson or unit. The key to the activity is encouraging students to return to previous entries to remember and build on the information. Student Journals have much more impact if the teacher can write occasional reactions to student entries.

For example, students review their earlier journal entries to access their background knowledge about the life cycle of a butterfly. After reading through what they have learned previously, students share with a partner and then bring the information into a whole class discussion. This previous learning becomes a foundation for beginning a new lesson on the life cycle of a frog. Connections between the two topics enhances student comprehension of life cycles.

SIOP Connection

Content Objective

Students will be able to connect their knowledge of one topic, such as the life cycle of a butterfly, to another topic, such as the life cycle of a frog.

Language Objective

▶ Students will be able to compare the life cycle of a frog to the life cycle of a butterfly using the word *because:*

"I think that the (frog's life cycle) _____
because the (butterfly's life cycle) _____."

▶ Students will be able to use the following sentence frames:

The life cycle of a frog includes the following phases: _____
_____
_____

The life cycle of a butterfly includes the following phases: _____
_____
_____

The phases are alike because: _____
_____
_____

The phases are different because: _____
_____
_____

Personal Dictionaries

■ **Grade Levels:** All

■ **Subject Areas:** All

■ **Grouping Configurations:** Individual, partners, small groups, whole class

Description

The purpose of Personal Dictionaries is to emphasize key vocabulary. Students create them as an individual vocabulary resource. The dictionaries can also be used as a spelling resource. Students add unknown words they come across while reading. The teacher works with students to clarify the words that they find.

The words in the dictionaries can be categorized by alphabetical order, subject, sound, morphological structure (such as past tense words), or by content and topic. Secondary teachers can assign personal word dictionaries that include content specific vocabulary. Very young children and beginning English speakers can be encouraged to use simple illustrations to represent words they are learning. In kindergarten and first grade, words can come from big books through a shared reading experience.

SIOP Connection

Content Objectives

▶ Students will be able to select and define words for ongoing vocabulary learning.

▶ Students will be able to make connections between previously learned vocabulary and vocabulary found in a new lesson and text.

Language Objectives

▶ Students will be able to write (or draw) a definition (or related meaning) for each new vocabulary word selected from text.

▶ Students will be able to describe the vocabulary connections using the following prompts:

"I remember this word from when we read about _____."

"I remember what this word means from when read about _____."

"I remember putting this word in my dictionary when we read about _____."

Four Corners Vocabulary

(Adapted from Deborah Short, Center for Applied Linguistics [CAL])

- ■ **Grade Levels:** All
- ■ **Subject Areas:** All
- ■ **Grouping Configurations:** Partners, small groups, whole class

Description

The purpose of Four Corners Vocabulary is to contextualize words through an illustration, a sentence, and a definition. Create a chart with (1) an illustration representing the vocabulary word, (2) a sentence that includes the word, (3) a definition of the word, and (4) the actual vocabulary word. The teacher may create the chart or upper grade students may create their own charts. Fold the chart paper in fourths so that students can only view one corner at a time. Start first with the illustration, then the contextualized sentence, then the definition, and finally show the class the actual vocabulary word (see example below).

Once completed, the Four Corners Vocabulary chart can be posted on the wall for further reference.

Illustration ❶	Sentence ❷
	The fluffiest clouds, that look like cotton, are called cumulus.
Definition ❸	**Vocabulary Word ❹**
A white billowy cloud type with a dark, flat base. (From the Latin cumulus, meaning "a heap.")	Cumulus

SIOP Connection

Content Objective

Students will be able to use an illustration, a definition, and a contextualized sentence to determine a matching vocabulary word.

Language Objectives

▶ Students will be able to read a contextualized sentence that includes a vocabulary word.

▶ Students will be able to read a definition for a vocabulary word.

Cognates

■ **Grade Levels:** All

■ **Subject Areas:** All

■ **Grouping Configurations:** Individual, partners, small groups, whole class

Description

Cognates are two words from two languages that have roots that look and sound alike and also have the same meaning. Cognates are generally easy to recognize, because they are spelled similarly. English and Spanish have many cognates. For Spanish-speaking students learning new content, understanding cognates helps them make connections to what they already know in their primary language. Pages 31 and 32 feature a few examples of the many cognates found in English and Spanish.

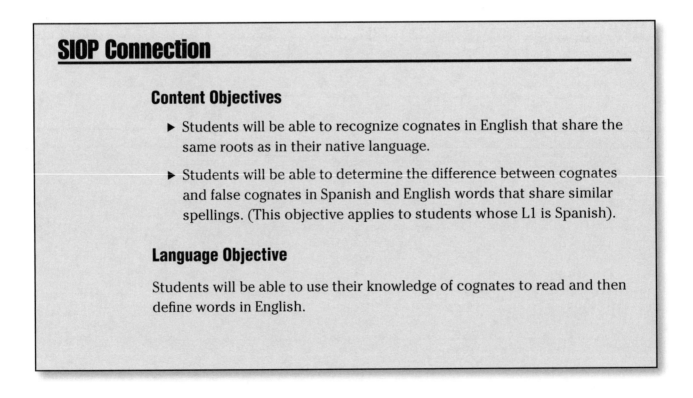

SIOP Connection

Content Objectives

▶ Students will be able to recognize cognates in English that share the same roots as in their native language.

▶ Students will be able to determine the difference between cognates and false cognates in Spanish and English words that share similar spellings. (This objective applies to students whose L1 is Spanish).

Language Objective

Students will be able to use their knowledge of cognates to read and then define words in English.

Cognate Examples

English	Spanish	Meaning
capital	capital	A city or town in which government leaders and others meet and work on behalf of a state, province, or country
cause	causa	A person or thing that makes something happen
artifact	artefacto	An object that is made and used by a particular group of people
colony	colonia	A place that is ruled by another country
communication	comunicacion	Sharing ideas with others orally or in writing
community	comunidad	A place where people live and work together
congress	congreso	A country's lawmakers
conservation	conservacion	Working to save natural resources to make them last longer
consumer	consumidor	A person who buys and uses goods and services
continent	continente	One of the largest bodies of land on the Earth
desert	desierto	A dry place; very little rain falls in a desert
diagram	diagrama	An illustration or flow chart that provides information about how something works
geography	geografia	The study of the Earth and its people
globe	globo	A model of the Earth
group	grupo	A number of people doing an activity together
history	historia	Events that have occurred in the past
independence	independencia	The freedom of people to choose their own government
invention	invencion	Something that has been created for the first time
island	isla	Land that has water all around it
leader	lider	A person who helps a group plan what to do

We must also be careful of what are known as false cognates. These are Spanish and English words that look very similar but they do not mean the same.

False Cognates

English	Spanish
agenda	orden del dia
appointment book	agenda
disturb	molestar
molest	accion indebido (sexual connotations)
embarrassed	avergonzado/a
pregnant	embarazada
excited	ansioso, nervioso, contento
	excitado/s (sexual connotations)
library	biblioteca
book store	libreria
minutes (from meeting)	acta (de una reunion)
portable	poratil
sympathy	pesame, condolencia
friendliness, congeniality	simpatia

Surprise Book

(Adapted from Bonnie Bishop, Long Beach Unified School District)

- ■ **Grade Levels:** K–5

- ■ **Subject Areas:** All

- ■ **Grouping Configuration:** Whole class

- ■ **Approximate Time Involved:** 5–10 minutes (depending on age and English proficiency of students)

Description

The Surprise Book activity is used at the beginning of a unit to activate students' background knowledge, while at the same time sparking their interest through the element of surprise. Choose a book that represents the unit theme and that has good visuals on the cover. Wrap the book in plain butcher or chart paper. At the beginning of the unit, present the book to the class, wrapped up in a way so that no part of the book is visible. Tell the students that they will slowly unwrap the book, taking off small pieces of paper at a time. Model the slow tearing away of the pieces and then ask students to take turns removing bits of the paper. As the paper is slowly torn away and the pictures on the cover of the book are revealed, encourage students to make predictions about the book's or topic's theme. Piece by piece their ideas will come together and at the end of the process they will know the theme of their next lesson or unit of study.

SIOP Connection

Content Objective

Students will be able make connections between their background knowledge and (the topic) of the Surprise Book.

Language Objective

Students will be able to speak in the future tense to predict what their next lesson or unit of study will be using the following sentence frames:

"I think we *will* learn about _____."

"I think we *are going to* study _____."

"I think this book *will be* about _____."

▪ SIOP Features ▪

10. Speech appropriate for students' proficiency level (e.g., slower rate, enunciation and simple sentence structure for beginners)

11. Clear explanation of academic tasks

12. A variety of techniques used to make content concepts clear (e.g., modeling, visuals, hands-on activities, demonstrations, gestures, body language)

Identifying Levels of Second Language Acquisition

■ **Grade Levels:** All

■ **Subject Areas:** All

■ **Grouping Configuration:** None (teacher assessment)

■ **Approximate Time Involved:** Ongoing process for every lesson

Description

It is very important that teachers determine the English language acquisition levels of their students. Once this is ascertained, teachers can make content comprehensible based on the language needs of each student. Teachers can also encourage students to increase their English proficiency by providing activities and opportunities for them to frequently use English. The following stages of language acquisition are fluid; that is, students don't move in concrete steps from one stage to the other. That said, it is helpful for teachers to understand how their students are progressing in acquiring English, and how they might respond to classroom instruction. Also, note that the titles for these stages vary. It is important to remember that learning a language is a process and that the more students use English (including listening to conventional English usage), the more proficient they will become.

Beginning (Pre-Production): Students have little comprehension of oral and written English, and they are unable to produce much, if any, oral or written English at this point. Teachers should provide abundant listening opportunities, use many physical gestures and movements to convey meaning, and include a great deal of context for shared reading and writing. If possible, partner beginning English speakers with others who speak the same primary language, and keep in mind that these students may understand more than they can communicate.

Beginning (Early Production): Students have limited English comprehension but they can give one or two word oral responses. For students learning to read in English, teachers can use predictable and patterned books and encourage them to label and manipulate pictures or fill in highly contextualized sentences.

Beginning (Early Speech Emergence): Students speak in simple sentences and can comprehend highly contextualized oral and written information. Teachers can expect these students to respond to simple open-ended questions. Teachers should continue to provide sufficient language development opportunities and include many activities that require students to read, write, listen, and speak. Teachers should encourage students to talk and write about personal experiences.

Intermediate (Early): Students have some proficiency in communicating simple ideas. They comprehend contextualized information. Teachers should continue to develop and extend sight word vocabulary. Teachers can encourage these students to expand on simple responses while developing critical thinking skills. These students should practice important grammatical structures to further their ability to generate and communicate ideas.

Intermediate: Students have proficiency in communicating ideas and they can comprehend contextualized information in English. Teachers should provide explicit instruction in figurative language, making predictions, using text features to read a book, and English grammar. These students can participate in generative activities that promote higher levels of thinking.

Early Advanced: Students can communicate well and have adequate vocabulary to achieve academically. They have good comprehension of information. Teachers should provide a variety of realistic writing and speaking opportunities. These students can be exposed to many different genres, more advanced grammatical structures, and activities to further practice critical thinking skills.

Advanced: Students have near native speech fluency and expanded vocabulary to achieve academically. They have very good comprehension of information in English. These students can lead group discussions, and they should be given opportunities to do presentations and to produce oral and written forms of communication. Teachers should continue to provide explicit grammar instruction.

Sample Responses

(Following are examples of divergent responses from the California Reading and Literacy Project)

Levels of English Proficiency:

- **Beginning:** "Brown bear."

- **Early Intermediate:** "The bear is brown. It has claws."

- **Intermediate:** "The bear has thick fur and sharp claws."

- **Early Advanced:** "The bear isn't a predator even though it has sharp claws and teeth."

- **Advanced:** "Before they hibernate for the winter, brown bears give birth to cubs."

Please remember that students at lower levels of English proficiency are not necessarily functioning at lower levels of cognitive ability. Frequently, these students are able to use higher level thinking skills in their primary language but have a more difficult time understanding the academic content and expressing their knowledge in English.

SIOP Connection

This information about students' levels of English proficiency does not lend itself to specific content and language objectives. Rather, it is information for teachers to use when planning instruction so that they can provide appropriate comprehensible input for English learners with varying levels of English proficiency.

Total Physical Response (TPR)

(Adapted from Asher, 1982)

- ■ **Grade Levels:** All
- ■ **Subject Areas:** All
- ■ **Grouping Configurations:** Individual, partners, small groups, whole class
- ■ **Approximate Time Involved:** Can be used to build background knowledge in beginning of lesson to clarify meaning during lesson input, and/or to review concepts

Description

TPR allows children to respond physically to a lesson by moving their bodies. Movement appeals to all students, but especially to kinesthetic learners. The teacher can use hand gestures, facial expressions, or whole body movement to illustrate key points in the lesson. The children then repeat the actions to make meaning of new words or concepts.

For example, if the teacher is teaching about orbit, rotation, and revolution of the planets, she can rotate and revolve her body around a light bulb representing the sun. Then she can give students a chance to rotate, revolve, and orbit around the light bulb. Another example is that students can use their hands as an "alligator" chomping the biggest piece when a teacher is teaching about the concepts of greater than and less than in a math lesson. TPR is fun and useful for all students; however it is vital for students with beginning language proficiency in English.

Signals are also a great way for students to interact with a lesson. Using hand signals for yes/no, true/false, I understand/I sort of understand/I don't understand responses, helps the teacher monitor the progress of the class and to make important decisions about how to proceed with lesson delivery.

SIOP Connection

Content Objective

Students will be able to use an appropriate physical response (e.g., hand signal) to represent a concept (e.g., if a number is greater than or less than another number).

Language Objective

Students will be able to use the language of greater than and less than to identify the symbol used to show the relationship between two numbers.

"_____ is greater than _____."

"_____ is less than _____."

Enlarged Adapted Text

- ■ **Grade Levels:** All

- ■ **Subject Areas:** All

- ■ **Grouping Configurations:** Individual, partners, small groups, whole class

- ■ **Approximate Time Involved:** Depends on length of text

Description

Textbooks can be intimidating and overwhelming for English learners. Text set in a small font appears alongside exciting pictures, captions, questions in sidebars, maps, and other graphics. Many students don't know where to focus their attention. By enlarging the font and adapting the text, the teacher can provide students with only the most important information.

Teachers simply type the text that students will be reading in an enlarged font and highlight 3–5 vocabulary words in bold type. (Often textbooks have as many as 15 vocabulary words in bold, which is too many words for ELs to focus on.) Students can use crayons or highlighters to identify words they recognize. They can use and change the enlarged text as they see fit.

Enlarged, adapted text lowers anxiety for new readers and students with lower levels of English proficiency. Teachers can also show students how to highlight or underline important concepts before they attempt to read the text. Students can draw their own pictures along the side or at the bottom of the page to help them negotiate meaning.

SIOP Connection

Content Objectives

▶ Students will be able to identify (with a highlighter) one key concept from each paragraph in enlarged, adapted text.

▶ Students will be able to identify (with a highlighter) and define three vocabulary words taken from enlarged, adapted text.

Language Objective

Student pairs will be able to orally paraphrase three key concepts after reading the enlarged, adapted text.

Vocabulary Cards and Vocabulary Flip Books

■ **Grade Levels:** All

■ **Subject Areas:** All

■ **Grouping Configuration:** Small group or whole class

■ **Approximate Time Involved:** 30 minutes

Description

As teachers, we often think of vocabulary cards for review. However, they can also be used to introduce or frontload vocabulary at the beginning of a lesson. This process helps students build on background knowledge and increases comprehension of the lesson or unit they will be studying.

There are many ways to make vocabulary cards. Cards can include sections for the word, picture, and/or definition. Cards can also include a place to use the word in a sentence. As a class spends time negotiating the meanings of key words before a lesson, they become familiar with the concepts they will discuss throughout the unit.

The class can also make flip books with 8.5" × 11" pieces of paper to display the vocabulary information. To make flip books, line up and arrange the paper so that you can see about an inch of each piece. Then fold all the papers in half. Put a paper clip on each folded half. Cut along the fold. Then, staple each section along the top. (See illustration on next page.) You will now have two flip books.

For example, students must create an eight-layer flip book with the first layer representing the title Taxonomy, and the subsequent seven layers representing the order of classification from smallest to largest: species, genus, family, order, class, phylum, kingdom. The flip book will act as a support for students. The flip book pages increase in size, just as the areas of classification do. For example, *kingdom* is written on the largest page of the flip book.

SIOP Connection

Content Objective

Students will be able to identify and describe the seven areas of classification within taxonomy.

Language Objective

▶ Students will be able to use comparative and superlative words to describe the order and size of the seven classifications in taxonomy: largest, larger, large, small, smaller, and smallest.

▶ Students will use ordinal numbers (first through eighth) to decide on which page of the flip book each classification should be placed.

FLIP BOOK

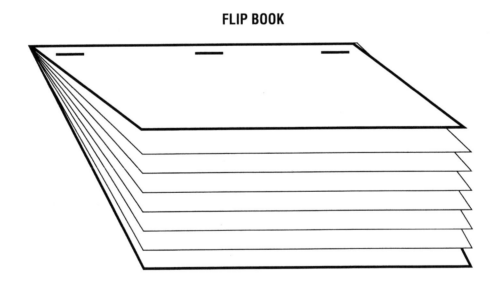

Homophones, Homographs, and Synonyms

- ■ **Grade Levels:** All

- ■ **Subject Areas:** All

- ■ **Grouping Configurations:** Individual, small groups, whole class

- ■ **Approximate Time Involved:** Ongoing process

Description

English learners will benefit from explicit instruction of homophones, homographs, and synonyms. Maintain a list of synonyms (different words that share the same meaning), homographs (phrases with words that are spelled the same but have different meanings; e.g., *duck under a gate, duck in the pond*), and homophones (words that sound the same but have different meanings and spellings; e.g., *sale* and *sail*). Posting these words gives students access to the "tricky" words that can be difficult for students learning English. Students can also organize these words in personal dictionaries or vocabulary notebooks. Simple illustrations for the words can serve as helpful mnemonics.

SIOP Connection

Content Objective

Students will be able to identify words that are synonyms, homographs, or homophones.

Language Objectives

- ▶ Students will be able to demonstrate that even though words may sound the same or share the same spelling, they may have different meanings.

- ▶ Students will be able to use sentence structures that allow them to compare and contrast word pairs, so that they may determine if the words are synonyms, homographs, or homophones.

  "_____ and _____ have the same meaning. They are synonyms."

  "_____ and _____ are spelled the same but they have different meanings. They are homographs."

  "_____ and _____ sound the same but have different meanings and spellings. They are homophones."

Idiom Match-Up

- ■ **Grade Levels:** 3–8

- ■ **Subject Areas:** Language arts

- ■ **Grouping Configuration:** Partners

- ■ **Approximate Time Involved:** 90 minutes to create game; 10–15 minutes for students to complete the game

Description

In addition to synonyms, homographs, and homophones, idioms and idiomatic expressions cause difficulty for English learners. Idioms can be recorded in a separate section of the personal dictionary or vocabulary notebook, and students can use simple illustrations to remember the words. Another fun way to have students practice their understandings of idioms is to play an idiom match-up game. Create a game board (colored poster board) and game cards (poster board cut into 2" × 2" squares). With a marking pen, divide the poster board into 2" × 2" squares. (Leave some space at the top for the game's name and playing directions.) In each square, write an idiom or idiomatic expression. On each card, write the meaning of the idiom. Ask student pairs to work together to match the meaning to the idiom. Illustrating the literal meanings of the idioms (e.g., a person who is frozen in an ice cube for the expression "Freeze!") and matching these to the idiomatic meanings also helps students remember the meanings. Students might also enjoy sharing some idioms and meanings in their native languages.

Following are some common English idioms and their meanings:

Idiom . . . . *Meaning*

Shake a leg! . . . . Hurry!

You'll catch more flies with sugar than vinegar . . . . Act nicely.

Hop to it! . . . . Get started on what you need to do.

Freeze! . . . . Do not move.

He's off the wall.. . . . . He behaves strangely.

She's over the top. . . . . .Her actions go beyond what people expect.

If you can't stand the heat,   Leave if you are uncomfortable
get out of the kitchen! . . . . with what people are saying or doing.

He has an eye for the girls.. . . . . He likes to flirt with pretty girls.

She has an eye for fashion.. . . . . She dresses very well.

SIOP Connection

Content Objective

Students will be able to match idiomatic expresses with their meanings.

Language Objective

Students will be able to explain the meaning of idiomatic expressions to a partner.

Taped Texts for Scaffolding

- ■ **Grade Levels:** All

- ■ **Subject Areas:** All

- ■ **Grouping Configurations:** Individual, partners, small groups, whole class

- ■ **Approximate Time Involved:** Depends on text; recording can be time consuming, but the completed tape can be used repeatedly

Description

Taping text is a great way to make content comprehensible. The reader (the teacher, student, or other individual) takes special care to use speech appropriate for students' proficiency levels, uses a slower reading rate, and clearly enunciates words. The reader adapts the text by finding synonyms for difficult words and deleting superfluous language, idioms, and figurative expressions that may confuse English language learners. Careful intonation and added inflection for dialogue helps to make these parts of the text more understandable. Using students or other people for readers provides varied inflections and intonations, thus multiplying the voices heard speaking English in the classroom. Perhaps most important, students can listen to the text multiple times to improve their comprehension and increase their English proficiency.

SIOP Connection

Content Objective

Students will be able to identify three key concepts related to (a topic) after listening to a story, article, or chapter.

Language Objective

Students will be able to orally explain to a partner why he or she thinks the identified three concepts are the most important in the story, article, or chapter.

Every Student Gets a Chance

■ **Grade Levels:** 2–12

■ **Subject Areas:** All

■ **Grouping Configurations:** Small groups, whole class

■ **Approximate Time Involved:** 5 minutes

Description

The teacher writes a new concept or idea on the board and reads it aloud. He or she then asks for a volunteer to read aloud what was just written. Then, instead of moving on to another concept or example, the teacher asks for a second volunteer to read aloud the same information. This continues so that each student who feels comfortable can choose to read the information aloud. Students who are at beginning levels of English proficiency will feel more comfortable repeating information after they have heard it spoken by each of their classmates. Note that in this activity, students are hearing the same input over and over from other students, rather than from the teacher, thus they hear other pronunciations, inflections, and intonations.

The activity is very effective for teaching, practicing, and reinforcing a concept such as place value and reading large numbers, and for helping students remember important definitions and vocabulary. For example, English learners need to learn the words *million, thousand, hundred, tens,* and *ones* in order to read the number 182,672,824. Teach students to identify the numbers in their sets of three:

182 (one hundred and eighty-two) *million*

672 (six hundred seventy-two) *thousand*

824 (eight *hundred* twenty-four)

Boost students' confidence by showing them that if they know their numbers from 1 to 999 they can essentially read any number simply by grouping them together in threes and adding the label of *million, thousand,* or *hundred*. Remember that students may already know these concepts from their schooling experiences in their native language. These students will just need to learn the English counterparts for the place value vocabulary. The repetition will enable them to learn the words more quickly.

SIOP Connection

Content Objective

Students will be able to read large numbers using the correct order and number terms.

Language Objectives

▶ Students will listen to the teacher and other students and then they will be able to repeat what they have heard.

▶ Students will be able to use the language of place value, including *million, thousand, hundred.*

Framed Outlines

- **Grade Levels:** 2–12
- **Subject Areas:** All
- **Grouping Configuration:** Small group or whole class
- **Approximate Time Involved:** Depends on text or lesson

Description

The teacher creates an outline of a text or of the lesson content, but leaves out some key information. Students complete the outline as they read through the text, listen to a mini-lecture, watch a video, and/or participate in the lesson in another way. Students can then refer to the framed outline during subsequent lessons and activities.

Framed Outlines provide an excellent opportunity to provide differentiated instruction. Some students may not need a partially completed outline or organizer; they may be able to create their own independently. Other students may need even more support than the partially completed outline. Support can be provided by including the first letters of key vocabulary and concepts and by including icons or simple illustrations as cues. Also, the teacher can work with a small group of students as they read through the text and complete the Framed Outline together.

SIOP Connection

Content Objective

Students will be able to take notes on a framed outline during a mini-lecture, text reading, or video viewing.

Language Objectives

▶ Students will be able to make meaningful guesses about the missing words in the framed outline.

▶ Students will be able to determine if the guessed word makes sense in the sequence of the outline.

Alternate Materials

■ **Grade Levels:** All

■ **Subject Areas:** All

■ **Grouping Configurations:** Individual, partners, small groups, whole class

Description

Use many materials to make content comprehensible to students. The more variation you find, the better you will be able to connect with different students' learning styles and background experiences. Following are examples of alternate materials:

1. Find pictures from books, magazines, travel brochures, and photographs.

2. Don't settle for black line masters of maps. Find authentic, real maps.

3. Use videos or snippets of videos to give picture support.

4. Bring in people from the community and experts to share collections and experiences.

5. Use realia (real objects) when possible. For example, when students are studying rocks, have them find rocks around the school or around their homes.

6. When students are literate in their primary language, provide access to the curriculum by letting them read about the content in their L1, if possible.

7. Have students draw pictures of their own experiences. They can make connections to the content in this way. Allow them to use their pictures to share and teach others in the class.

8. Find clip art on your computer that goes with the unit.

9. Use literature, poetry, and music about content concepts.

10. Field trips and excursions help students create first-hand knowledge about a subject.

11. Whenever possible, encourage students to do hands-on activities.

12. Find and/or make timelines that display chronological events.

13. Bring in foodstuffs to display content concepts. For example, make pancakes with added foods (e.g., chocolate chips) to show the metamorphic process of melting, changing size, shape, and color.

14. Let students create classroom materials. Bring in modeling clay to illustrate the layers of the earth's surface.

15. Use various graphic organizers to help students visually organize and remember new information. Once they have organized information into a graphic organizer, they can use visual cues to recall information.

SIOP Connection

Content Objectives

▶ Students will be able to demonstrate their understanding of *greater than, less than,* and *equal to* by placing Cuisinaire rods in an equation with symbol cards >, <, and =.

▶ Students will be able to compute simple numerical equations using the symbols > and <.

Language Objective

Students will be able to read and write equations with number words and the terms *greater than, less than,* and *equal to.*

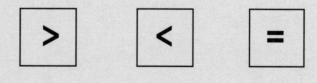

▪ SIOP Features ▪

13. Ample opportunities provided for students to use learning strategies

14. Scaffolding techniques consistently used, assisting and supporting student understanding (e.g., think alouds)

15. A variety of questions or tasks that promote higher-order thinking skills (e.g., literal, analytical, and interpretive questions)

Directed Reading-Thinking Activity (DRTA)

(Adapted from Stauffer, 1969)

- ■ **Grade Levels:** All (Directed Listening-Thinking Activity can be used for K–1)
- ■ **Subject Areas:** Language arts (or any subject area when a piece of fiction is used)
- ■ **Grouping Configuration:** Whole class
- ■ **Approximate Time Involved:** Depends on the length of the text

Description

For more than 30 years, teachers have used the DRTA to assist students in learning how to strategically comprehend narrative (fiction) text. Throughout the reading of a story or book, the teacher and students stop periodically and contemplate predictions about what might follow logically in the next section of the text. The teacher begins the lesson with a question about what the class members think the story or book will be about based on the title. As students respond, other questions follow, such as:

- "With a title like _____, what do you think this story will be about?"

- "Let's read to find out."

- Revisit predictions: "Did _____ happen? If not, why not?"

- "What do you think is going to happen next? What makes you think so?"

- "Where did you get that idea?"

- "What made you think that?"

It is important that teachers revisit previous predictions after reading chunks of text so that students come to understand how predictions (and their confirmation or disconfirmation) impacts their comprehension. Students can vote on which predictions are most likely and explain why, as they focus their thinking on character (and author) motivations, problems characters face, reasons for characters' behaviors, and how the plot unfolds. Note that DRTA is also effective for longer novels, with chapter-to-chapter discussions focusing on what students think will happen, what really happened, and why.

SIOP Connection

Content Objective

Students will be able to generate predictions about (a story or book's events), justify their predictions, and confirm or disconfirm their predictions after reading the text.

Language Objective

Students will be able to use the following sentence frames when making predictions, justifying predictions, and confirming or disconfirming predictions:

"I predict that _____ will happen, because _____."

"I wish to change my prediction to _____, because _____."

"My prediction was confirmed when _____."

"My prediction was disconfirmed when _____."

Questioning Prompts for Different Levels of Language Acquisition

(Adapted from Long Beach Unified School District)

■ **Grade Levels:** All

■ **Subject Areas:** All

■ **Grouping Configurations:** Individual, partners, small groups, whole class

■ **Approximate Time Involved:** Ongoing process in every lesson

Description

Teachers need to vary their questioning prompts based on the different levels of language acquisition represented in their classrooms. The sample prompts listed below elicit varied responses that are sensitive to students' English proficiency levels. Remember that students at lower levels of language proficiency are not necessarily at lower levels of cognitive ability. Many times, they are able to use higher level thinking skills in their primary language but have a hard time understanding the academic content or expressing their knowledge in English.

It takes skill and practice to craft higher level questions and activities that allow students to use whatever language they have so they can participate in appropriate grade level tasks. The following suggestions are provided to help teachers see how students' responses can become more complex as they gain additional English proficiency. When activities vary from literal to interpretative to applied, teachers can create heterogeneous groups with students of different English proficiency levels. These groupings can provide appropriate and necessary scaffolding for students who are beginning speakers of English.

- **Beginning Pre-Production:** Ask students to point to something or touch the answer. Have them signal by clapping or physically moving items in a lesson.

- **Beginning Early Production:** Ask students questions that require a yes/no, either/or, or one to two word answer.

- **Beginning Early Speech Emergence:** Students can respond in simple sentences. Ask questions such as, "Which animal was your favorite in the story? Why?"

- **Early Intermediate:** Students can generate and respond in simple sentences. Ask questions such as, "Tell me about your story" or "What did you do to solve that problem?"

- **Intermediate:** Students can generate and respond in simple connected narratives. They can answer questions such as, "What happened in the story?" and "How will the story end?"

- **Early Advanced:** Students can respond in sequential narrative, justify, summarize, evaluate, and synthesize information. They can compare items and answer "why" questions.

- **Advanced:** Students who have near native speech fluency can be asked to explain in detail cycles and processes.

SIOP Connection

Content Objective

Students will be able to respond to teacher-generated content questions appropriate to their levels of English proficiency.

Language Objective

Students will be able to use gestures, words, phrases, and sentences to answer teacher-generated questions.

Canned Questions

(Adapted from Karen Mettler, Prescott Senior Elementary School, Modesto, CA)

- ■ **Grade Levels:** 2–12
- ■ **Subject Areas:** All
- ■ **Grouping Configuration:** Whole class
- ■ **Approximate Time Involved:** 20 minutes

Description

The teacher writes various questions on strips of paper related to a particular topic. The questions range from lower to higher level thinking skills. The questions ask students to demonstrate (according to Bloom's Taxonomy):

- *Knowledge* by defining, locating, underlining, labeling, or identifying things.
- *Comprehension* by describing, summarizing, explaining, or paraphrasing.
- *Application* by computing, building, or giving an example.
- *Analysis* by categorizing, classifying, comparing and contrasting.
- *Synthesis* by combining, creating, designing, or predicting.
- *Evaluation* by concluding, defining, justifying, or prioritizing.

All question strips are placed in a can. Students are grouped in pairs or small groups to lower anxiety and to scaffold. The teacher draws out the questions, one by one, and students work together to answer them. Occasionally, the teacher may choose to pull a question and based on its difficulty (in terms of the English proficiency required for response), select individual students to answer. With this variation, all students gain exposure to questions of varying cognition levels, although they are only responsible for answering the questions that are appropriate for their level of English proficiency.

Students may also submit questions to the question can (individually or in groups). These can be drawn for the other students to answer. Teachers can teach students how to ask higher order questions using QARs (Question-Answer Relationships [Raphael, 1984]). Three levels of questioning are represented by the following:

Literal: "Right There." The answer to a question can be found right on the page. (Example: What is a rabbit's resting place in the wild called?)

Interpretive: "Think and Search." The answer must be determined by reading between the lines; it is not explicitly stated in the text. (Example: "Why do you think it is called a farm?")

Applied: "On Your Own." The answer isn't stated either explicitly or inferentially, but comes from a reader's own experiences or background knowledge. (Example: What are some names of other animals' resting places?")

For children in grades K–2, two levels of questions can be taught:

Literal: "On the page."

Interpretive/Applied: "In my hand."

SIOP Connection

Content Objective

Students will be able to respond to questions written at various cognitive levels on (a topic).

Language Objectives

▶ Students will be able to display their knowledge of (the topic) by using complete sentences when answering a question.

▶ Students will be able to answer questions on increasingly sophisticated levels of cognition using the following prompts:

Knowledge: The definition of (topic) is _____.

Comprehension: (Topic) can be explained as _____.

Application: An example of (topic) is _____.

Analysis: (Topic) can be compared to _____.

Synthesis: If I create a diagram of (topic), I will include _____ in my diagram.

Evaluation: We can conclude that (topic)_____.

Anticipation/Reaction Guide

(Adapted from Readence, Bean & Baldwin, 2001)

- ■ **Grade Levels:** 2–12
- ■ **Subject Areas:** All
- ■ **Grouping Configurations:** Small groups, whole class
- ■ **Approximate Time Involved:** 10 minutes before lesson and 10 minutes after lesson

Description

Create agree/disagree or true/false statements based on the text and/or content concepts to be studied. Before reading, students (individually) read through the statements and mark their responses on the left side (Anticipation) of the statements. Students then share responses with a partner and make predictions about what they will be learning, setting their purpose for reading. After reading the text, students mark their responses to those same statements on the right side (Reaction) of the statements. The class then discusses why the text reading changed some of their responses. Anticipation/Reaction Guides can also be used to preview and review information on an upcoming unit. For very young children or beginning speakers of English, simple illustrations can support the reading of the guide statements.

Topic: Natural Disasters Agree (A) or Disagree (D)

Anticipation   Reaction

_____ Hurricanes cause the most damage of
any type of natural disaster in the U.S. . . . . _____

_____ Insurance companies should not be held
responsible for covering damage to homes
and businesses from natural disasters. . . . . _____

_____ People should be able to rebuild their homes
in the same places even though the location is
commonly in the path of hurricanes. . . . . _____

_____ The U.S. government must refit all buildings
and highways that are earthquake-prone. . . . . _____

SIOP Connection

Content Objectives

▶ Students will be able to agree or disagree about Anticipation statements written about (a topic).

▶ Students will be able to make predictions about what they will learn by reading about (a topic).

▶ After reading, students will be able to review their earlier predictions and clarify questions or misconceptions about (a topic).

Language Objective

Students will be able to use the appropriate language to confirm or disprove predictions, using the following sentence frames:

"I think this is true because _____."

"I think this is false because _____."

"I confirmed my prediction when I read _____."

"I disproved my prediction when I read _____."

"I agree with the statement because _____."

"I disagree with the statement because _____."

Progressive Maps

(Adapted from Shelly Frei, Long Beach Unified School District)

- ■ **Grade Levels:** All
- ■ **Subject Areas:** History and social studies (also other subjects)
- ■ **Grouping Configurations:** Small groups, whole class
- ■ **Approximate Time Involved:** Ongoing process

Description

Progressive Maps encourage students to visually organize old and new information. A unit begins with a directed drawing on a map.

For example, for a unit on Native Americans, students might add grass and streams to an empty map (on chart paper), to show that no one has lived there yet. They might add various landforms (desert, forest, mountain range). As students learn more, new information is added to their maps (or map, if it is a whole class activity). A picture of the buffalo that came from the north can be added, as well as drawings of the people that followed. Markers can be added to indicate where various tribes settled.

The same maps can be brought out again as the class begins to study the westward movement of the European settlers in the United States so that students can build on their prior knowledge. The information on Native Americans will already appear on the map. Students can add exploration ships, new colonies, and draw in covered wagons that traveled nearby the Native American settlements. As the map goes through changes, students receive visual support to help them use higher thinking skills as they evaluate changes, hypothesize possible causes and effects, and defend opinions about what happened. When a timeline and specific labels are added to the map, students can connect the visual representations to the vocabulary and concepts.

SIOP Connection

Content Objective

Students will be able to visually represent their knowledge of (topic) through drawings on a Progressive Map.

Language Objectives

▶ Students will be able to describe what they have visualized about (topic) through the use of key phrases, including:

"In my head I see_____."

"I picture_____, because _____."

"I visualize_____, because_____."

▶ Students will be able to use sequence words that represent time:

"In the 15th century, _____."

"What followed was_____."

"But today, _____."

"In the future, _____."

T-Chart Graphic Organizer

■ **Grade Levels:** All (teacher records information for lower grades)

■ **Subject Areas:** All

■ **Grouping Configurations:** Individual, partners, small groups, whole class

Description

A T-Chart is a graphic organizer intended to help students classify information. It is important to scaffold this process. At first, the teacher models by drawing a large T-Chart on chart paper. Next, the teacher writes on the T-Chart while the class brainstorms information about a topic. Then, a teacher asks partners to fill out a T-Chart to classify brainstormed information. Finally, students are asked to individually fill out a T-Chart. A teacher can further scaffold this activity by providing students with information students then classify into the two lists. Eventually students are asked to generate their own items. A triple T-Chart includes three categories (sometimes called an M-Chart).

For example, the general topic is animals and the two categories are wild animals and domesticated animals (or animals that are pets). Students brainstorm examples and explain their rationale for placing each animal in the appropriate category.

ANIMALS	
Wild	**Domesticated**

SIOP Connection

Content Objectives

▶ Students will be able to classify (a topic) on a T-Chart.

▶ Students will explain their rationale for placing example of (a topic) in a particular category.

Language Objective

Students will be able to use classifying language when determining which examples belong to each category and justify the reasons for their classification, using sentence frames such as:

"I think _____ belongs to this group, because _____."

"I am not sure in which group this _____ belongs, because _____."

Split Page Note Taking

- ■ **Grade Levels:** 3–12
- ■ **Subject Areas:** All
- ■ **Grouping Configurations:** Small groups, whole class
- ■ **Approximate Time Involved:** Depends on text length and difficulty

Description

Before the lesson, students divide a piece of paper in half. The teacher directs them to copy down a few questions about the topic on the left side of the paper. As the class reads through the text (individually, in partners, or with a group), each student writes notes, answering the questions on the right side. After practicing this technique several times, students can be taught how to write their own questions by previewing the text and/or by using the headings and turning them into questions. After much modeling of the activity, students will be able to create the questions independently.

It will be helpful to teach students (especially English learners) the following:

- A "who question" indicates that the answer will include a person's name.
- A "what question" indicates that the answer will include a description of an action.
- A "when question" indicates that the answer will include a time frame for something happening.
- A "where question" indicates that the answer will include a place where something happened.
- A "why question" indicates that the answer will include an explanation of a person's actions.
- A "how question" indicates that the answer will include a description of a process.

When students have completed a Split Page Note Taking activity for an article or chapter, the notes/answers they have written on the right side of the paper can also be used as a foundation for summary writing and for reviewing the material prior to a quiz or test. Please keep in mind that students who have learned how to ask and answer questions in their native language need to learn the corresponding English vocabulary for questioning. Students who have not developed literacy in their native language will need much more explicit instruction and modeling of the process of asking and answering questions.

SIOP Connection

Content Objectives

▶ Students will be able to answer questions regarding (topic) through Split Page Note Taking.

▶ Students will be able to identify the type of information they are looking for based on key words in the questions (*who, what, when, where, why*).

Language Objective

Students will be able to respond correctly to questions by finding the key words *who, what, when, where, why*.

Stop and Think

(Adapted from Shelly Frei, Long Beach Unified School District)

- **Grade Levels:** Developing readers (may be of varying grade levels)
- **Subject Areas:** All
- **Grouping Configurations:** Individual, small groups, whole class
- **Approximate Time Involved:** 5 minutes

Description

Proficient readers accomplish many tasks as they read through a short passage in a text. They make predictions, infer information, visualize a scene, and generate new questions. Usually, they do these tasks without even realizing that they are doing them. Beginning readers often don't realize that they are supposed to do this and they solely focus on decoding the words. These students are confused when their classmates can answer questions after reading a text, while the beginning readers don't understand what happened in the story. As teachers, we tell our struggling readers to reread, but they often do so with the same results.

Teachers can do a number of things to scaffold these skills and strategies for beginning and developing readers. First, be aware of all that you do "in an instant" of reading. Explicitly explain these different skills and strategies to students. During read-alouds, model the processes one at a time in a think-aloud (e.g., "When I read this, I think of _____.").

During shared and guided reading, give a hand or sound signal that tells students to "stop and think." During this time, they are to stop reading, practice the skill or strategy they are learning that day, share their thinking with a partner, and then continue reading. Explicitly teach thinking strategies such as: *imagine, remember, think of a question, predict, pretend, recall, listen, look, think about, visualize, solve mentally, summarize to yourself,* or *make an inference* (or *infer*). It is important to model what you mean by each of these terms; again, think-alouds provide a great mental-model for students. They learn what you do when you engage in these varied thinking and reading strategies.

SIOP Connection

Content Objectives

▶ Students will be able to make personal connections during the reading of (a text) as they practice the Stop and Think strategy.

▶ Students will be able to use a signal to demonstrate that they are taking the time to Stop and Think.

Language Objective

Students will be able to articulate how they are making connections to what they know and what they have experienced, using the following sentence frames:

"When I read _____ it made me remember when _____ ."

"This part of the (story, article, chapter) makes me think of a time when _____ ."

You Are the Teacher!

- **Grade Levels:** 3–12
- **Subject Areas:** All
- **Grouping Configuration:** Small groups within whole class setting
- **Approximate Time Involved:** 45–60 minutes

Description

For this activity, students need explicit instruction in how to move around the classroom appropriately. You Are the Teacher encourages students to learn important information by allowing students to teach other class members. After reading and/or researching a selection of text, student small groups create a chart, using words, illustrations, or a graphic organizer to arrange the information they have learned. The posters are then attached to the walls around the classroom.

Within each group, members decide who will remain to teach the next group and who will move on to the next poster. Students may choose a number from 1–100, do rock-paper-scissors, or choose pre-ordained colored strips from an envelope (one color stays, the other moves on). Beginning English speakers should be paired with more fluent speakers, whether they stay or move on.

Students moving to the next poster should proceed in a clockwise rotation. Students who remain with the poster teach the new students about the information on the chart or poster. At each rotation, students should again decide who stays and who rotates. Eventually, students will return to their original posters. It is important that the teacher ask each final group to report the key information so the "playing telephone" effect is minimized. While it is important for students to have an opportunity to share information and interact with each other, it is critical that the content information be taught correctly by the students.

SIOP Connection

Content Objectives

▶ Students will be able to create posters containing pictures and information about (a topic).

▶ From the posters, students will be able to share information with fellow students that they have learned about (a topic).

Language Objective

Students will be able to use language to clarify what is being taught to them, what they understand, and what they don't understand, as they move from group to group, using the following sentence frames:

"I understand that this is about _____."

"I don't understand _____."

"I have a question about _____."

"Can you explain _____ to me again?"

Value Line

(Adapted from Temple, 1998; and Vogt, 2000)

- ■ **Grade Levels:** All
- ■ **Subject Areas:** All
- ■ **Grouping Configurations:** Small groups, whole class
- ■ **Approximate Time Involved:** 15 minutes

Description

A Value Line requires students to apply knowledge that they have just learned, draw on past learning and experiences, and take a position (i.e., state their values) about difficult topics. For example, high school students might study a piece of pending legislation intended to establish a parent's right to know over a teenager's right to privacy. After reading and discussing the legislation, two students "in character" serve as advocates for each position, urging class members to take one of the advocated positions (parents' rights or students' rights). The mock debate between the two opposing positions (the ends of the Value Line) incorporated clear arguments and specific support for the respective viewpoints.

When the advocates finish arguing their positions, the other students take a position on the spectrum, with one end of the Value Line representing the parents' right to know and the other end of the line representing the students' privacy rights. Before they assume their places on the line (an imaginary line that bisects the classroom), students negotiate with those around them in order to determine where they belong. While doing so, the students also attempt to persuade other class members to move toward one position or the other. In the end, each class member must articulate why he or she chose a particular spot and how people standing to the left or the right held different perspectives on the topic.

Value Line can be modified by having students assume an identify other than their own (e.g., historical figures or literary characters). Figures or Characters take a stand on the line about a topic or event relevant to them. All students assume a character's identity as they take a stand, defend their positions, and try to persuade other characters to move toward one end or the other. For example, in the classic story "The Lottery" by Shirley Jackson (1982), the ends of the line would represent "yes" or "no" positions in answer to the question: "Should the town's annual lottery continue?" Students assume the role of the townspeople arguing for one position or the other until everyone has taken a stand.

Younger students can be involved in this same type of activity using stories, decisions characters must make, and choices. You can coach with questions such as, "What do you think you would do?" "What do you think Ramona should do?" Students can begin to see how their own choices might be similar to or different from those of their favorite characters in picture books.

Some teachers believe that English learners cannot participate in an activity such as Value Line. While the ELs may need scaffolding to understand the content concepts, as good thinkers they can certainly "take their stand" along the line, and with a partner, explain why they have assumed their stance.

SIOP Connection

Content Objective

Students will be able to demonstrate their knowledge and understanding of (a topic) by assuming a place along a continuum of perspectives (the Value Line).

Language Objectives

▶ Students will be able to orally explain to students around them why they have assumed the position they have on the Value Line, using the following sentence frame: "I am standing here on the Value Line, because _____."

▶ Students will be able to try to convince other students to change their position by using the following sentence frame: "I think you should move over here, because _____."

Adapted Venn Diagram

- ■ **Grade Levels:** K–12 (teacher can complete the Diagram on chart paper for K–1)
- ■ **Subject Areas:** All
- ■ **Grouping Configurations:** Individual, partners, small groups, whole class
- ■ **Approximate Time Involved:** 15 minutes

Description

Many teachers use a Venn Diagram to compare and contrast information. A Venn includes two intersected circles. Information about two different concepts, ideas, or objects is written in each circle. Where the circles intersect, students write information about what is the same about the two concepts, ideas, or objects. The adapted Venn Diagram uses intersected squares instead of circles. The squares are arranged side by side, with the second square slightly lower (see diagram below). This configuration gives more room to write the examples of how the two things are the same. Another adaptation is to use sticky notes for the Venn, because they are movable and can be shifted around when new learning takes place or thinking changes.

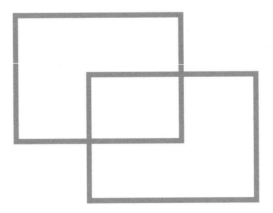

SIOP Connection

Content Objective

Students will be able to compare and contrast the work of two authors.

Language Objective

Students will be able to use key vocabulary to articulate differences and similarities between the authors (similar, both, different, but):

"They are similar, because they both _____."

"They are different, because _____."

"_____ writes about _____,
but _____ writes about _____."

▪ SIOP Features ▪

16. Frequent opportunities for interaction and discussion between teacher/student and among students, which encourage elaborated responses about lesson concepts

17. Grouping configurations support language and content objectives of the lesson

18. Sufficient wait time for student responses consistently provided

19. Ample opportunities for students to clarify key concepts in L1 as needed with aide, peer, or L1 text

Is It Complete?

(Adapted from Angie Medina, Long Beach Unified School District)

- **Grade Levels:** 1–4
- **Subject Levels:** All
- **Grouping Configurations:** Individual, partners, small groups, whole class

Description

The purpose of Is it Complete is to encourage interaction among students while encouraging and promoting individual thought and the use of complete sentences. Students (individually, in pairs, or as a group) are asked to respond to a particular question. They must answer in complete sentences. After the question is asked, the teacher allows some quiet thinking time. A sentence frame should be visible to students who need the extra support. Visual aids and posted vocabulary related to the content concepts help students think of sentences. Once students have produced a complete sentence they should put their thumbs up together to signal to the teacher that they are finished. The individuals' sentences can be shared with partners and/or small groups and the partners' or groups' complete sentences can be shared with the entire class, if desired.

SIOP Connection

Content Objective

Students will be able to share their knowledge about a topic through sharing complete sentences with a partner.

Language Objectives

▶ Students will be able to create singular and plural sentences when discussing a topic.

▶ Students will be able to add an *s* or *es* to the end of words to make plurals, and use the word *are* as the verb to describe them:

"The _____ is for _____."

"The _____*s* are for _____."

"The _____ is important because _____."

"The _____*s are* important because _____."

Dinner Party

(Adapted from Vogt, 2000)

- ■ **Grade Levels:** All (for K–2 use a birthday or tea party)
- ■ **Subject Areas:** Language arts, social studies, science, math
- ■ **Grouping Configuration:** Small groups
- ■ **Approximate Time Involved:** 1–2 periods for planning

Description

The idea for this activity came from a final exam that one of the authors (MaryEllen) had when she was a senior in high school way back in the early '60s! The course, English literature, was taught by an extraordinary teacher, Mary McNally, and for the semester exam she asked students to respond to the following prompt:

> "Suppose you could have a dinner party for eight British authors or poets that we have studied. Who would you invite? Why would you select them? What would be the seating order of the guests at your table and why would you place them in that order? What do you think the guests would talk about during dinner? Include specific references to the authors' lives and works in your response."

The purpose of Dinner Party (or Birthday Party) is for students to act out the above questions by assuming personas, such as characters in novels or short stories, authors or poets, historical figures, scientists, artist, politicians, or military leaders. For example, Alexander the Great might be engaged in conversation with Abby Hoffman, while General George Patton argues the finer points of military strategy with Jane Fonda. Although scripts can be written, improvisation is more interesting and fun. However, success depends on the age of the students, their content knowledge, and language proficiency. During each Dinner Party, students must include specific content and respond, in character, to each other as realistically and accurately as possible. It is important to stress that knowledge of the figures' lives, accomplishments, flaws, and works must be used to inform the performance.

Young students can have a tea or birthday party and include their favorite characters from stories or nursery rhymes. When you model how a character might act at a tea party prior to students deciding on the "guests," they are more likely to understand the purpose of the activity.

SIOP Connection

Content Objective

Students will be able to assume the persona of a character (fictional or real) and represent his or her unique history, personality, and characteristics.

Language Objective

Students will be able to talk about (perhaps with a partner) their characters' accomplishments and other personal facts during a pretend dinner party (or birthday or tea party).

Group Response With a White Board

■ **Grade Levels:** All (for K, use pictures or illustrations, numbers, or words in a multiple choice format)

■ **Subject Areas:** All

■ **Grouping Configurations:** Individual, small groups, whole class

Description

The purpose of Group Response With a White Board is to encourage interaction between class members while promoting individual thought. Students are grouped heterogeneously and each group is given a number. Each student in the group has a piece of paper and pencil and each team has a white board and marking pen. The teacher asks a question about a topic the class has been studying.

After allowing sufficient wait time, the teacher asks the students to individually jot on their paper their responses to the question, even if it's a best guess. The team members then share their responses with each other on cue from the teacher. Together, they determine the best response and a recorder writes it on the white board. It is important that all team members help each other by making sure that all students know the answer. When teams have written on the white boards, the teacher spins a spinner or rolls a die. According to number, a group holds up the white board to share the answer with the rest of the class. The team must support its answers. If the answer is wrong, it is important to emphasize that the *team* response was incorrect. Spin or roll the die to select another team until the correct answer appears. The team (and class) then discuss the question and answer so that everyone is able to answer it correctly. Team points can be awarded, if desired. Group Response With a White Board is a wonderful way for students to assess student understanding of key concepts in a low-risk environment.

SIOP Connection

Content Objectives

▶ Students will be able to work with teammates to devise the best possible answer for a question related to (a topic) being studied.

▶ Students will be able to evaluate the team member's individual responses for accuracy.

Language Objectives

▶ Students will be able to defend their team's choice in choosing a particular response.

▶ Students will be able to use language to defend and explain their thinking:

"We agree that _____ is the best answer, because _____."

"We came to consensus that _____ is the best answer, because _____."

Reader-Writer-Speaker Response Triads

(Adapted from Barbara H. Formoso, Gunston Middle School, Arlington, VA)

- ■ **Grade Levels:** All (for K–1, use illustrations for jobs)
- ■ **Subject Areas:** All
- ■ **Grouping Configurations:** Partners, small groups, whole class

Description

The purpose of Reader-Writer-Speaker Response Triads is to encourage interaction between class members while promoting individual thought. Students need to be grouped in triads. The key to this activity is that each triad can only use one paper and only one writing utensil (pencil, pen, or marking pen). Each student takes a turn reading, writing (recording) the triad's answer, and speaking (reporting) the answer. Everyone in the triad helps each of the other members: the reader reads an article, chapter, or adapted text; the writer (recorder) writes or draws the group's response; the speaker (reporter) shares the group's responses with the other class members. This activity can be used for brainstorming (e.g., naming all the proper nouns they know), for review (e.g., writing all the fact families they know), or even for drawing the cycle of something (e.g., the water cycle). This can also be used for test preparation.

Barbara Formoso makes simple construction paper "tents" in three different colors. Each group has one Reader tent, one Writer tent, and one Speaker tent. These tents are rotated among students within the triad based upon the lesson's objectives.

SIOP Connection

Content Objective

Students will be able to work in a group and share their knowledge about (a topic, e.g., math fact families) orally and in writing with their team.

Language Objective

Students will be able to read, write, listen, and speak about a topic.

Inside-Outside Circle

(Adapted from Kagan, 1994)

- ■ **Grade Levels:** All
- ■ **Subject Areas:** All
- ■ **Grouping Configurations:** Partners, small groups, whole class

Description

The purpose of Inside-Outside Circle is to encourage interaction and oral language development. The class is divided into 2 groups. Half of the class forms a circle looking out (the inside circle). The other half of the class stands in front of someone in the inner circle (to form the outside circle). (Younger students often do better in this activity if they are seated in the two circles.) The students are asked a question or are directed to perform a task. The students in the inner circle answer first while the outer circle listens. Then the outer circle responds while the inner circle listens. When each has finished, students can give a signal (e.g., thumbs up) to indicate that they are finished. Once both have shared, the teacher can give a signal (e.g., ringing a bell). The inner circle stays in place while the outer circle rotates one person clockwise.

For example, as students rotate through the Inside-Outside Circle, the students of the inside circle share a piece of writing while the students of the outside circle act as the editors. With each rotation, the editors have a particular task, perhaps to check punctuation. The outside circle continues to rotate while helping to revise the stories that are being read by the inside circle. The next day the roles change and the inside circle becomes the editors while the outside circle shares their writing.

SIOP Connection

Content Objective

Students will be able to edit and revise their writing with the help of a partner.

Language Objective

Students will be able to help revise another student's writing by using *praise* and *suggestion* sentence frames such as:

"I like how you _____."

"Did you think about _____?"

"The best part is how you _____."

Find Your Match

- ■ **Grade Levels:** All

- ■ **Subject Areas:** All

- ■ **Grouping Configurations:** Partners, small groups, whole class

Description

The purpose of Find Your Match is to encourage interaction between class members while reading and producing oral language. Each student is given an index card with information on it that matches the information on another student's card (e.g., words and definitions; antonyms or synonyms; generals and battles; characters and story titles; math problems and solutions, etc).

In the first step, students mix with each other, reading aloud the information on their cards. After students have had several opportunities to share their information, the teacher calls time. At that point, students are to find their matches by *describing* (not reading) what is on their cards. For example, if students are learning about geometric shapes, one student might have *parallelogram* on his card and another might have the definition of parallelogram on hers. While searching for their matches, the first student must try to define parallelogram while the second student sees if *parallelogram* is written on his or her card. When the two students with a match find each other, they move to the side of the room until everyone is finished. At that point, all partners read both of their cards to the rest of the class.

SIOP Connection

Content Objective

Students will be able to match words and/or concepts about (a topic, e.g., microsope and its parts).

Language Objectives

▶ Students will be able to orally read the word(s) on their cards to other students.

▶ Students will be able to describe the concept that is written on a card to another student.

"I have the _____ (e.g., microscope piece). Its job is to _____."

Jigsaw What You Know

■ **Grade Levels:** All

■ **Subject Areas:** All

■ **Grouping Configurations:** Small groups, whole class

Description

The purpose of Jigsaw What You Know is to encourage interaction between class members through learning about a topic, classifying the topic within a whole, and then teaching others about the topic as one dimension of the whole. Choose a topic that has two to four possible dimensions or qualities (e.g., animals or food). Assign each dimension to a specific area in the classroom. Label the areas with pictures or words. (Assign students an area through index cards that have words or pictures related to one of the particular dimensions.) Place resources related to the topic in each designated area. Tell students to use the resources to learn about the particular dimension and decide how to best represent the dimension for their peers.

For example, the topic of study might be the food pyramid. The class would be divided into six groups (protein, fats, dairy, fruits, vegetables, grains). Each student's index cards would picture or label a different food. Students go to the food group that is appropriate for the food pictured or labeled on their cards. After each group reads together an article about their food group (e.g., protein), they use the information to create a small poster that explains their food group (e.g., what they are, how they contribute to good health, examples of various types of this group, etc.). Each group will teach the rest of the class about their food group and add their poster to the whole class chart on the food pyramid.

SIOP Connection

Content Objectives

▶ Students will be able classify foods into one of six food groups.

▶ Students will be able to create a poster that will be used to teach the other five teams about their food group.

Language Objectives

▶ Students will be able to use an adjective to describe the food that is on their index cards.

▶ After generating a class list of adjectives that describe foods, students will be able to describe their food to their team using an adjective before the noun, while describing which food group it belongs to.

"The _____ (adjective) _____ (noun) belongs to the _____ group." (Examples: "The yellow banana belongs to the fruit group." "The creamy yogurt belongs to the dairy group.")

Gallery Walk

- **Grade Levels:** 2–12

- **Subject Areas:** All

- **Grouping Configurations:** Individual, partners, small groups, whole class

Description

The purpose of Gallery Walk is to encourage interaction between class members while promoting written and oral language. Students are placed in groups of four or five. Multiple charts are posted around the room with a particular question or topic written across the top. Each group begins at a different chart, focusing on its particular topic or question. Each group lists two or three ideas or responses on the chart, using a marking pen of a different color from the other groups. Groups are given three or four minutes at each chart paper, and then they rotate to the next chart, reading other groups' contributions and adding additional information with their colored marking pen. Groups may question or react to information written by previous groups. The process continues until all groups have responded to all chart papers. Then groups return to their original chart, read what the others have written, and summarize orally all of the responses for the class members. At this point, questions may be answered, points are clarified, and the teacher may lead a whole class discussion of the topic.

SIOP Connection

Content Objective

Students will be able to work in a group and respond in writing to questions and comments about (a topic) that are written on chart paper.

Language Objectives

▶ Students will be able to ask questions in writing about (a topic) in response to what other students have written on the chart paper.

▶ Students will be able to orally summarize all of the information about (a topic) that was written on their chart paper.

Take a Stand

- **Grade Levels:** All

- **Subject Areas:** Social studies (including current events), language arts, literature, health

- **Grouping Configurations:** Individual, partners, small groups, whole class

Description

The purpose of Take a Stand is for the teacher to quickly assess students' comprehension of a lesson and for the students to practice their listening skills. The teacher makes a statement to the students related to a current event, a story or novel, an issue related to students' health, etc. After making the statement, the teacher permits quiet think time. When the teacher says, "Take a Stand," the students stand up if they agree with the statement and stay seated if they disagree.

Take a Stand can also be a team activity. First, the team discusses the statement made by the teacher and then they come to consensus on whether they will sit or stand. On cue, the entire team stands or stays seated. Teams must be prepared to explain their rationale for agreeing or disagreeing.

An adaptation to this activity is to allow students to create the statements used for agreeing or disagreeing and ask the rest of the class to respond.

SIOP Connection

Content Objective

Students will be able to agree or disagree with positions (e.g., with positions of politicians related to a current event) and provide a rationale for their decision.

Language Objective

Students will be able to respectfully agree or disagree with other class members' perspectives about (a topic), using sentence frames:

"I respectfully disagree with _____, because _____."

"I agree with _____ because _____."

Frozen Moment

(Adapted from Schultz, 1998; and Vogt, 2000)

- ■ **Grade Levels:** All
- ■ **Subject Areas:** Language arts, social studies, science
- ■ **Grouping Configurations:** Individual, partners, small groups, whole class

Description

Begin by reading a piece of literature connected to content, such as Allen Say's *Grandfather's Journey* (1993), a beautiful book about a Chinese immigrant family. After reading the story, distribute to each group (four or five students) a piece of paper that has a three or four sentence scene taken from the story. Give each group a few minutes to plan a re-creation of the scene in pantomime. However, the scene must be delivered with absolutely no movement, similar to a tableau, and each person in the group must take a role. The roles may be characters (such as the grandfather or grandmother) or stage props (such as the cherry tree, ship, or waves). After sufficient time to practice, students create their "frozen moments" while the rest of the class members close their eyes. When ready, class members view the scene and attempt to identify the particular scene that is being portrayed.

After the students have viewed the scene for a few minutes, the teacher joins the performers and touches one of the actors, who then "comes to life." In character, this student describes what he or she is thinking or feeling at that moment. For example, the ship crossing the ocean might say, "I am so tired. I've been to sea now for weeks and I've been tossed about by huge waves and fierce storms. I must stay afloat and save my passengers." The teacher ends the soliloquy by again tapping the student, who then returns to the fixed, still position. Other players in the scene may be tapped until class members have correctly identified the scene that is being performed.

It's important to let several cast members come to life during the re-creation, even if the rest of the students think they can identify the scene. Much of the fun in this activity is watching the "frozen moment" come to life, and this part of the process should not be rushed.

SIOP Connection

Content Objectives

▶ Students will be able to read about a scene in a story and with peers and re-enact the scene as a tableau, including key characters, events, and settings.

▶ Students will be able to watch a tableau and determine which scene the actors are portraying.

Language Objectives

▶ Students will be able to orally describe the roles they are playing in the tableau by assuming a character or element of the setting.

▶ Students will be able to listen to characters in the tableau in order to determine the scene they are portraying.

▶ Students will be able to "come to life" as a character or other figure and improvise what the character or figure might say at that moment in time.

You Are There

(Adapted from Vogt, 2000)

- ■ **Grade Levels:** 4–12
- ■ **Subject Areas:** Social studies, math, language arts, science
- ■ **Grouping Configurations:** Small groups, whole class

Description

This activity is based upon the classic television program *You Are There,* hosted by Edward R. Murrow, in which characters involved in actual historical events were interviewed about their involvement and participation in the event. The re-creations were historically accurate, and the historical figures came alive for viewers.

In preparation for You Are There in the classroom, groups of students conduct research on the event they will be portraying. Once they have completed their research, they select a character that played a crucial role in the event. The students in this research group then write interview questions and responses that an interviewer will use during the dramatic re-enactment.

For example, students could interview Sacajawea, the Shoshone guide and interpreter who accompanied Lewis and Clark on the expedition, or they might interview the Wright brothers upon their arrival at Kitty Hawk, North Carolina. Both the interviewer and the interviewee are apprised of all questions and responses prior to the performance.

You may wish to add another dimension to this activity, especially if you are working with older high school students: audience members can direct unrehearsed questions to the central character. Obviously, all students, including the interviewee, must have a thorough knowledge of the event for this to be a successful activity.

SIOP Connection

Content Objectives

▶ Students will be able to demonstrate their understanding of (a person or historical event) by creating interview questions and responses.

▶ Students will be able to convey the essence of the (person or historical event) through an interview that is performed for peers.

Language Objectives

▶ Students will be able to write interview questions.

▶ Students will be able to create appropriate responses to the interview questions.

Great Performances

(Adapted from Vogt, 2000)

- ■ **Grade Levels:** 3–12
- ■ **Subject Areas:** Social studies, math, language arts, science
- ■ **Grouping Configurations:** Small groups, whole class

Description

In this activity, students act out significant events either in pantomime or improvisation, such as Alexander Graham Bell's first use of a telephone, Henry Ford's realization that automation could increase the production of Model T's, or Neil Armstrong's first steps on the moon. Depending on the content and grade level, students select either an event that is very well known or one that is interesting and important but not as famous. In pairs, students conduct research on their selected topic, learning as much as possible about the specific sequence of events leading up to the Great Performance.

With an activity such as this, it may be easier to start students with pantomime, then move to improvisation with speaking, then move on to writing and performing brief scripts. Students including English learners who are shy about speaking in front of peers can effectively and creatively pantomime events and situations. Through pantomime, students learn how to communicate with facial expressions, body language and position, and movement.

SIOP Connection

Content Objective

Students will be able to act out a sequence of events that led to a great moment in history.

Language Objectives

▶ Students will be able to plan the Great Performance by using sequence words, such as *first, then, next,* and *finally.*

▶ Students will be able to improvise a scene and speak as a character in an historical event.

Practice/ Application

▪ SIOP Features ▪

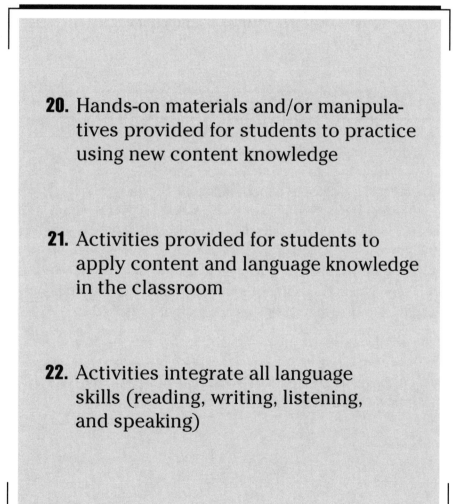

20. Hands-on materials and/or manipulatives provided for students to practice using new content knowledge

21. Activities provided for students to apply content and language knowledge in the classroom

22. Activities integrate all language skills (reading, writing, listening, and speaking)

In the Loop

(Adapted from Peggy Senneff, Long Beach Unified School District)

- ■ **Grade Levels:** All
- ■ **Subject Areas:** Math, science
- ■ **Grouping Configuration:** Individual, partners
- ■ **Approximate Time Involved:** 10 minutes (depending on amount of time teacher decides to allow and how many examples students are required to give)

Description

The purpose of In the Loop is to encourage student interaction while allowing the use of manipulatives (which can later be eaten) for the more tactile students. Pairs are given a piece of paper for a work site and a medicine cup (which can usually be purchased from the stock catalog) of generic loops or round oats cereal. Classes are given a problem, from simple addition to cell construction, which they must demonstrate with the loops. Students should be allowed time to look at other responses and explain their own before loops are eaten or another problem is given. For example, students working with partners can decide how to place the loops to mimic the construction of a cell.

Note: *Teachers can purchase large boxes of generic loops, which can be stored for use at any time. Teachers may want to hand out baby wipes or anti-bacterial hand lotion before giving cereal to students. Students then write about the process that they went through.*

SIOP Connection

Content Objective

Students will be able to demonstrate the construction of a cell through the use of loops.

Language Objective

Students will be able to use prepositions and prepositional phrases when describing to their partners how and where to place the loops: *next to, on top of, between, under, near, behind,* and *below.*

BINGO

- ■ **Grade Levels:** All

- ■ **Subject Areas:** All

- ■ **Grouping Configuration:** Individual

- ■ **Approximate Time Involved:** 15 minutes

Description

The purpose of BINGO is to provide students with a hands-on method of practice with words or facts. Students are asked to fold a blank piece of newsprint into 9 (3×3) or 16 (4×4) squares. The teacher displays 10–20 vocabulary words or math facts. The students fill in the squares in a random order so that no two papers are identical while the teacher passes out paper squares (which can be collected and saved for the next BINGO game), or cereal loops which can be eaten after the lesson. While the game is in session, the teacher does not call out the exact word or fact the students have written, but a definition or related fact. Students must find the match and cover the square.

For example, if students have written *cell,* the teacher says, "It is a very small unit of living matter." If the students have written *7* the teacher says, "It is the square root of 49." Students can also say aloud the definition so that other class members have to determine the word that is being defined. This activity may be carried out over the course of two days. On the first day, students answer each clue and write it in a random square. On the second day, students play the game.

SIOP Connection

Content Objective

Students will be able to identify, define, and use (vocabulary related to the content of the topic).

Language Objectives

▶ Students will be able to determine if (a vocabulary word) is a common noun or a proper noun and use either lowercase or uppercase letters (e.g., for a lesson on the solar system, vocabulary words could include *rocks, sun, moon, planets, orbit, satellite, Pluto, Venus, Earth, Mars,* and *Saturn*).

Are You Sleeping?

(Adapted from Peggy Senneff, Long Beach Unified School District)

- **Grade Levels:** K–5
- **Subject Areas:** All
- **Grouping Configurations:** Partners, small groups, whole class
- **Approximate Time Involved:** 15–20 minutes (depending on how much of the language is scaffolded by the teacher)

Description

The purpose of Are You Sleeping is to encourage students to practice what they are learning through familiar melodies. For example, most students know the melody to "Are You Sleeping?" With assistance from the teacher, they summarize content information into four or eight phrases that fit the melody. The lyrics can be written on charts so that on subsequent days the whole class can sing them together. Students can use a variety of resources (texts, poems, vocabulary lists, picture books) to assist them in creating the songs.

For example, in a unit on weather, the teacher can brainstorm, post, and discuss weather-related terms such as *stormy, blowing, cloudy, rain, cold, hot,* and so forth. Using the tune, "Are You Sleeping?," students might create a song like the following:

"Is it stormy?

Is it stormy?

Yes, it is!

Yes, it is!

See the wind is blowing,

See the leaves are falling,

See the clouds,

Hear the rain."

Additional vocabulary related to the weather could be substituted for additional verses. Note that some English learners, depending on their native country, may not be familiar with nursery rhymes and folk songs that are indigenous to the United States. Remember to teach the original song (e.g, "Are You Sleeping?") prior to replacing the lyrics with those generated by the class.

SIOP Connection

Content Objective

Students will be able to create songs based on the content concepts related to (a topic).

Language Objective

Students will be able to generate vocabulary related to (a topic) and create phrases that can be sung to a familiar melody.

Poetry and Patterns

(Submitted by David J. Larwa)

■ **Grade Level:** 5–12

■ **Subject Areas:** Math, science

■ **Grouping Configuration:** Small groups

■ **Approximate Time Involved:** One class period (depending on the background of the students)

Description

The purpose of this activity is to review and reinforce vocabulary words in mathematics and science. Using vocabulary words, students in cooperative groups write one Haiku for each group member. The Haiku can be written as a true or false statement. The pattern for Haiku:

- Five Syllables
- Seven Syllables
- Five Syllables

Begin by reviewing a unit's vocabulary words. Have students write out their reasoning in true or false form. Then tell each group to write Haikus for all members. Groups share poems with the class and the class determines whether they are true or false.

True Example

(Vocabulary word: variable, a letter that represents a number)

A variable

Any letter (x) will do

An unknown number

(Vocabulary word: variable expression, an equation containing a variable)

The equation is

Variable expression

2x = 6

False Example

(Vocabulary word: ratio, a comparison of two numbers or quantities)

Ratios compare

Too, a colon, or fraction

Can be simplified

Next Steps: Tanka

Tanka is a Japanese poetic form that consists of 31 syllables (5-7-5-7-7). It is the most fundamental poetic form in Japan since Haiku is derived from it. Develop and write a Tanka after the study of a science topic as in the one below from earth science.

ring of fire earthquake

they have taken many lives

tsunami water

too far away to notice

death and damage at my door

For more ideas of using poetry in the content areas read *Practical Poetry: A Nonstandard Approach to Meeting Content-Area Standards* by Sara Holbrook. (2005). Portsmouth, NH: Heinemann. ISBN 0-325-00767-5.

SIOP Connection

Content Objective

Students will be able to recognize and evaluate the operational definitions of mathematical (or science) terms.

Language Objective

Students will be able to write Haiku, a Japanese poetic pattern of three lines, each with a specific number of syllables.

Go Graphic for Expository Texts

- ■ **Grade Levels:** 3–10
- ■ **Subject Areas:** All
- ■ **Grouping Configuration:** Partners, small groups, whole class
- ■ **Approximate Time Involved:** 10–20 minutes

Description

The purpose of Go Graphic is to encourage organized thought processes through the use of graphic organizers that are related to a variety of text structures. The first step in the process is to teach students that authors write expository text in ways that often reflect the content they are describing. Graphic organizers that mirror how the text is written can help students better understand how to read and learn the material. Model how to identify the type of text structure by showing many different examples. Then, one by one, introduce the graphic organizers that best match the text examples.

After introducing graphic organizers to the class, ask students (in partners or groups) to select the appropriate organizer (based on the structure of a text the group reads together) and use it to organize the content. After students have completed the organizers, ask them to write a summary paragraph about the text.

For example, the most common text structures found in expository texts (nonfiction and informational texts) include:

Explanation (main idea and supporting details)

Cause and Effect

Comparison and Contrast

Sequence or Chronological

Problem/Solution

Description

(See pages 118–123 for examples of each organizer.)

SIOP Connection

Content Objective

Students will be able to depict the life of a character in graphic and written form.

Language Objective

Students will be able to use regular and irregular past-tense verbs (e.g., *born, lived, graduated, married, had, invented, died*) to describe the different phases of a character's life that are represented on the timeline.

Explanation: Main Idea and Supporting Details

This organizer also can be used to help students learn how to write a simple paragraph. The Main Idea becomes the topic sentence and Conclusion becomes the concluding sentence.

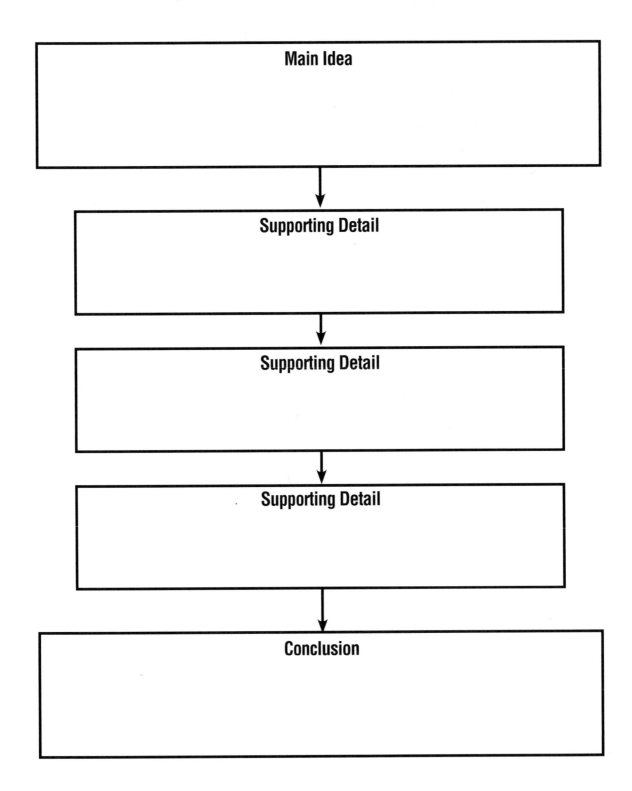

Main Idea

Supporting Detail

Supporting Detail

Supporting Detail

Conclusion

Cause and Effect

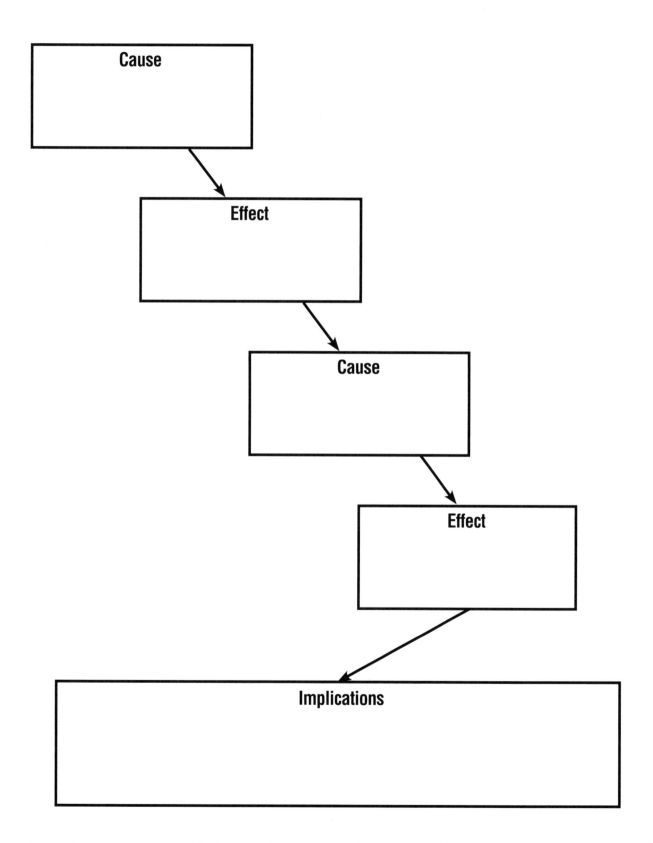

Cause

Effect

Cause

Effect

Implications

Compare and Contrast

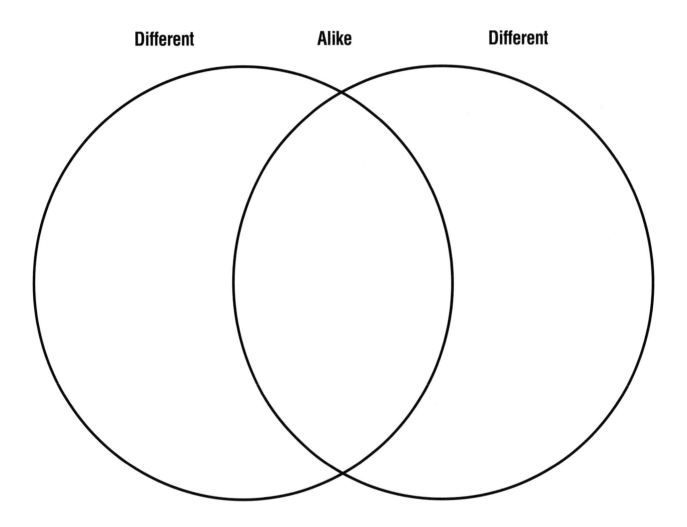

Different   **Alike**   **Different**

Sequence or Chronological

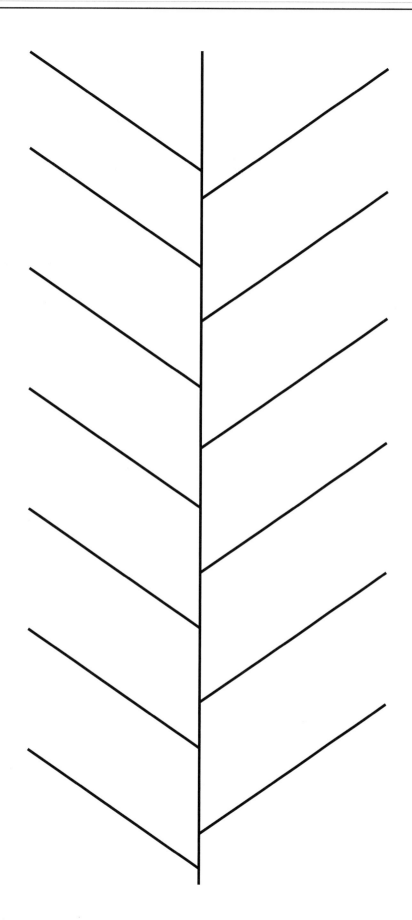

Problem/Solution

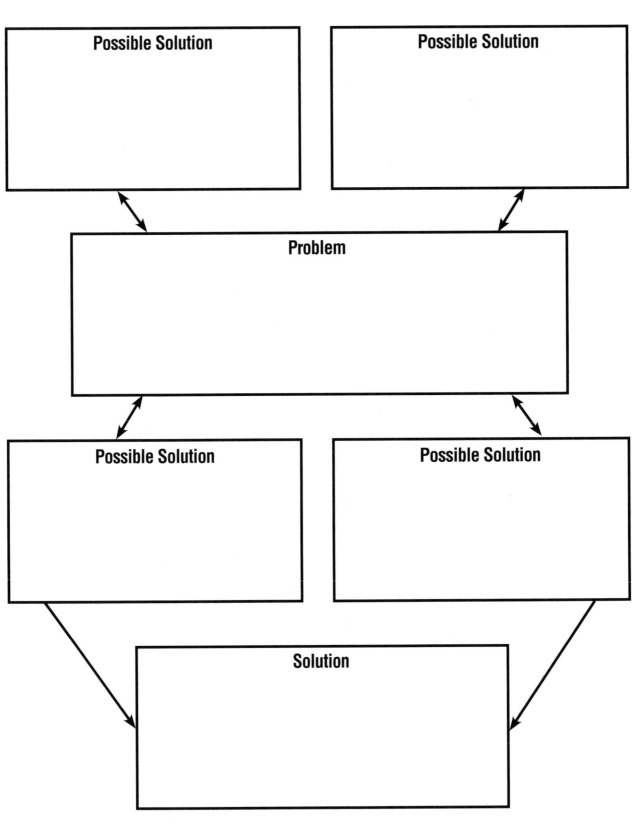

Description

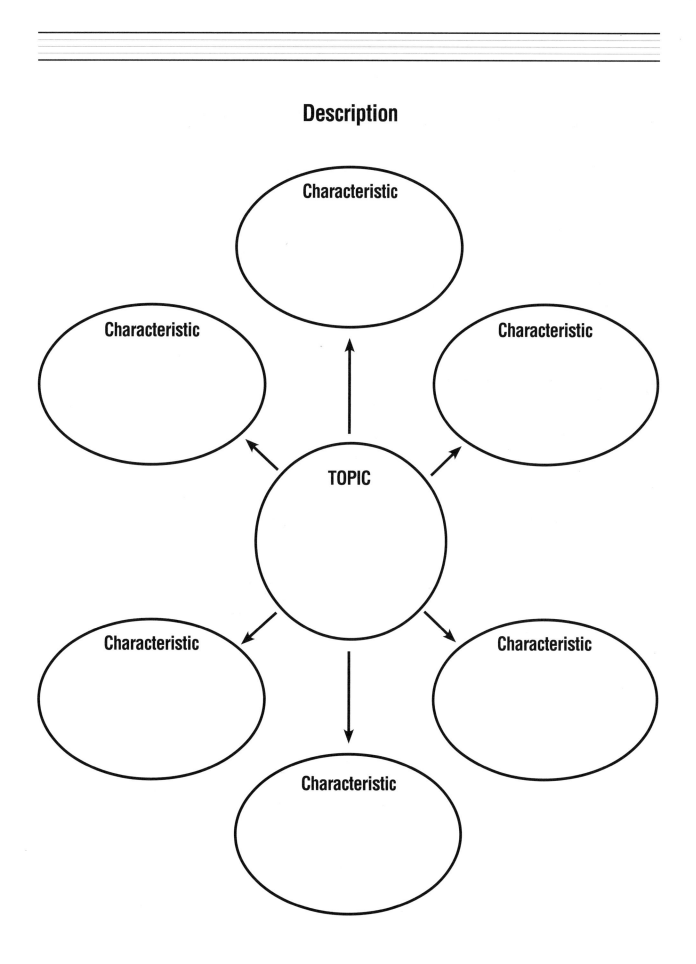

Plot Chart and Short Story Flow Chart

(Plot Chart adapted from Barbara Schmidt and Macon, Buell & Vogt, 1991. Short Story Flow Chart from author, MaryEllen Vogt)

- ■ **Grade Levels:** K–2 for Plot Chart and 3–10 for Short Story Flow Chart
- ■ **Subject Areas:** Language arts and other subjects when stories (narrative texts) are read
- ■ **Grouping Configurations:** Partners, small groups, whole class
- ■ **Approximate Time Involved:** 10–30 minutes (depending on the length of story)

Description

In the previous activity (Go Graphic), teachers were encouraged to show students how to organize information using specific graphic organizers for six common expository text structures. The Plot Chart and the Short Story Flow Chart have the same purpose (organizing information), but they are specifically intended for narrative (fiction) text, particularly picture books or short stories. It is important to model how to use the charts several times before students complete them independently. The Short Story Flow Chart also works well as a pre-writing activity when students are learning to write their own short stories. They complete the Flow Chart prior to writing out their stories.

SIOP Connection

Content Objectives

▶ After reading (or listening to) a short story, students will be able to re-create the sequence of the story on a Plot Chart.

▶ After reading a short story, students will be able to identify the story's elements (title, author, setting, main characters, problem, and sequence of events) using a Short Story Flow Chart.

▶ Students will be able to evaluate the extent to which they enjoyed the short story, providing a rationale for their rating (using the Short Story Flow Chart).

Language Objectives

▶ Students will be able to summarize and sequence a short story plot using the prompts on the Plot Chart.

▶ Students will be able to write in three sentences the beginning, middle, and end of a short story they have read on the Short Story Flow Chart.

▶ Students will be able to describe the main character of a short story with adjectives other than *nice* and *good*.

Plot Chart

Somebody

wanted

so

but

so

In the end,

(Adapted from Barbara Schmidt and Macon, Buell, & Vogt, 1991)

Short Story Flow Chart

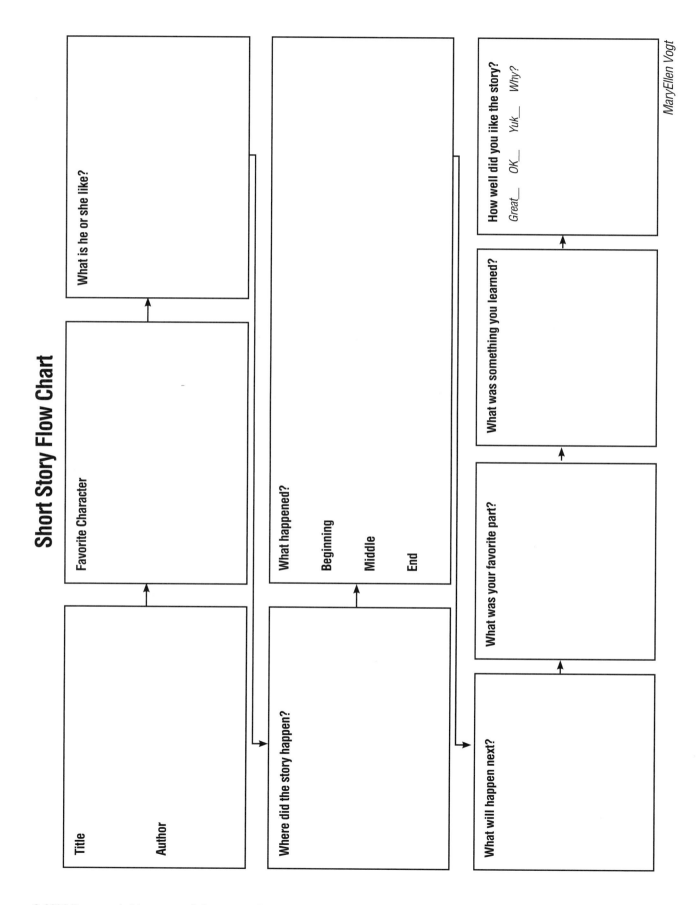

Title

Author

Favorite Character

What is he or she like?

Where did the story happen?

What happened?

Beginning

Middle

End

What will happen next?

What was your favorite part?

What was something you learned?

How well did you like the story?
Great___   OK___   Yuk___   Why?

MaryEllen Vogt

The Frame-Up

(Adapted from Long Beach Unified School District)

- ■ **Grade Levels:** 2–8
- ■ **Subject Areas:** All
- ■ **Grouping Configuration:** Small groups of 2 or 4
- ■ **Approximate Time Involved:** 15 minutes for main activity plus 5 to 10 minutes for sharing (after activity or on the next day)

Description

The purpose of The Frame-Up is to help students sort the components of a concept (e.g., four habitats that make up a region, four components of a healthy diet, four types of mammals, or four types of vegetables). The teacher distributes to each group (four or five students) a sheet of construction paper and another piece of construction paper to be used as a frame. The central topic is written in the center of the construction paper. Students take turns passing the frame around as each student asks (interviews) the others about ideas for filling in one side of the frame. The second student asks the group for ideas on filling in the second side of the frame and so on. The third student asks the group for ideas on filling in the third side of the frame, etc. (For example, students might write the name of a region [e.g., Northwest] in the center of the frame. Then they might pass the frame around the group, writing about four habitats related to that region on the four sides of the frame.) Later, students can be assigned to write what they learned about the topic, using the frame as an organizer. The frames are presented to the other teams to share the information gathered.

Students should have access to various classroom resources to facilitate the completion of the four sides of the frame. The Frame-Up works as a culminating activity when information has been gathered previously.

SIOP Connection

Content Objective

Students will be able to orally and in writing share information about four components of (a topic).

Language Objectives

▶ Students will be able to use comparative adjectives in the creation of their frames about (a topic) and four of its components.

▶ Students will be able to add *-er* and *-est* to adjectives to compare and contrast their descriptions of the four different components.

Piece O' Pizza

- ■ **Grade Levels:** 2–12
- ■ **Subject Areas:** All
- ■ **Grouping Configurations:** Partners, small groups
- ■ **Approximate Time Involved:** 15 minutes

Description

The purpose of Piece O' Pizza is to demonstrate how parts make up a whole. This activity is ideal for following up a jigsaw reading activity during which each group of students has been given a section of an article or chapter to read. It is also helpful to use Piece O' Pizza when teaching about a concept, idea, or object that has many parts. A large circle is cut into slices with each slice passed out to a small group of students. Groups decorate the slice with information bits and illustrations (when appropriate). Later the pizza is reassembled as the groups to share their information. Students can then choose or be assigned a slice to write about or to illustrate in more detail.

For example, each group could be assigned one battle of the U.S. Civil War to depict and explain on one slice of the pizza. The groups should include important details relevant to the respective battles. The information will be shared by the team with the whole class and then placed together with the other pieces of information to form the Civil War Pizza.

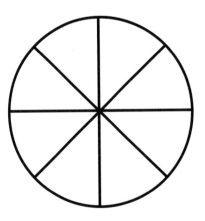

SIOP Connection

Content Objectives

▶ Students will be able to describe eight components of (the topic).

▶ Students will be able to summarize information about (one component, such as battles of the Civil War).

Language Objective

Students will be able to use past tense verbs to describe (one component, such as battles of the Civil War).

Virginia Reel

- ■ **Grade Levels:** All
- ■ **Subject Areas:** All
- ■ **Grouping Configuration:** Partners
- ■ **Approximate Time Involved:** 10 minutes

Description

The purpose of Virginia Reel is to give students a chance to review or practice newly learned information. Students form two lines facing each other. One line of students has a question, statement, or problem written on the card, along with the answer (e.g., a spelling word, a math equation or a word problem, a clue to a story character, a vocabulary word and definition, a description of an historical occurrence, etc.). One student reads the word, equation, or clue to his or her partner, waits for a response, and then checks to see if the response is correct. At the teacher's cue, one line then shifts one partner to the right while the person on the end goes around to the beginning of the line to meet a person without a partner. After the students with cards have asked several students, they hand the cards to their partners who then move again to the right and ask a new partner. The activity can be repeated a number of times until students are exposed to as many of the cards as possible. Following the activity, the teacher and students should discuss areas of confusion that arose during the Virginia Reel so that clarification can be made for the entire class.

For example, during a Virginia Reel, one half of the students have cards with an idiom on one side and its meaning on the other. Students holding the card read the idiomatic expression to a partner and the partner guesses the true meaning of the phrase. The first student then confirms the student's guess or tells the correct meaning. The students then exchange cards and move on to another partner.

SIOP Connection

Content Objective

Students will be able to identify (words, idiomatic expressions, equations, etc.), and guess their meaning.

Language Objective

Students will be able to use the following sentence frames when making guesses about the meaning of idiomatic expressions:

"I think _____ means _____."

"My guess is that _____ means _____."

"My idea is that _____ means _____."

"My thought is that _____ means _____."

Numbered Heads Together

(Adapted from Kagan, 1994)

- **Grade Levels:** 3–12
- **Subject Areas:** All
- **Grouping Configuration:** Small groups within a whole class setting
- **Approximate Time Involved:** 30–45 minutes

Description

The purpose of Numbered Heads Together is to provide students with practice in reviewing material prior to an exam (or other assessment) and to encourage the sharing of information so that all students can master the content and language objectives related to a topic being studied. Students are grouped heterogeneously (four or five students per group) with varied language acquisition and ability levels. Once grouped, they count off so that each student has a number. The teacher displays prepared questions at different levels of difficulty on a transparency or PowerPoint. As the questions are revealed, each group discusses possible answers and finds consensus on one answer. The teacher then spins a spinner and calls out a number from 1–4 or 1–5. If the number is 2, all the students who are number 2 in each group will stand up and give their group's answer. Though everyone in the group is responsible for the answer, only one person in each group is chosen to report the group's response.

While Numbered Heads Together is highly effective, it takes some time to teach the procedures. Once students understand how to participate, however, the possibilities are endless. Numbered Heads Together can be used for "finding the one right answer," such as solving math equations. It can also be used for answering open-ended questions where every group may have a different answer. It is very effective for standardized test preparation, where students have cards that say a, b, c, or d. The person whose letter is called displays that group's answer and their group's rationale.

SIOP Connection

Content Objectives

▶ In groups, students will be able to come to consensus on a response to a question (or statement) about (a topic).

▶ Students will be able to provide a rationale for the group's response to the question about (a topic).

▶ Students will be able to evaluate how well prepared they are as a group to answer questions and discuss (the topic).

Language Objectives

▶ In a group, students will be able to discuss questions and responses related to (the topic).

▶ Students will be able to come to consensus about their responses by respectfully agreeing and disagreeing with each other, using the following sentence frames:

"I disagree with your answer, because I believe it should be _____."

"The correct answer is _____, because _____."

"I agree you have the correct answer because, _____."

Vocabulary Go-Fish

(Adapted from Judy Senneff, Long Beach Unified School District)

- **Grade Levels:** K–8

- **Subject Areas:** All

- **Grouping Configuration:** Small groups

- **Approximate Time Involved:** 5–10 minutes for preparation and as much time as desired to play the game.

Description

The purpose of Vocabulary Go-Fish is to increase students' vocabulary in a cooperative setting. The teacher may create any number of vocabulary cards, such as a simple word on one side of the card with a corresponding picture on the other side. More challenging cards might have a word on one side and a definition, synonym, antonym, illustration, or sentence on the other. Each group receives a paper bag that holds slips of paper with the vocabulary words on them. The students are numbered within each group. When the teacher calls a number, the student with that number in each group will Go Fish for a vocabulary word. The teacher then tells the students what response to give for the words they drew (e.g., a synonym, sentence, or definition). The student who has gone fishing reads the word and gives the information, then checks for accuracy by looking on the back of the card. Students' responses may be given orally or in writing.

Older students can be enlisted to create the cards for younger students, and then play Go Fish with them. Beginning English speakers can develop their language proficiency by creating and illustrating cards with vocabulary words and then playing Go Fish with younger students.

SIOP Connection

Content Objectives

▶ Students will be able to match (vocabulary words to their definitions, synonyms, antonyms, etc.).

▶ Students will be able to define (vocabulary related to a topic).

Language Objectives

▶ Students will be able to provide (definitions, antonyms, synonyms, etc.) for (vocabulary words), using the following sentence frames:

"_____ is an antonym for _____."

"_____ is a synonym for _____."

"_____ is a definition for _____."

▶ Students will be able to find their matching cards by using the following sentence frame:

"My card says _____."

"What does your card say?"

"Do you want to trade?"

"Do we have a match?"

Lesson Delivery

▪ SIOP Features ▪

23. Content objectives clearly supported by lesson delivery

24. Language objectives clearly supported by lesson delivery

25. Students engaged approximately 90% to 100% of the period

26. Pacing of the lesson appropriate to the students' ability level

Stand Up–Sit Down

(similar to Take a Stand)

- ■ **Grade Levels:** K–12
- ■ **Subject Areas:** All
- ■ **Grouping Configuration:** Small groups or whole class
- ■ **Approximate Time Involved:** 5–15 minutes (depending on number of questions posed)

Description

The purpose of Stand Up–Sit Down is to give students the opportunity to respond to true/false statements through movement, while the teacher monitors student comprehension during lesson delivery. The teacher makes a statement about the content being taught and students must decide if it is true or false. If a student decides the statement is true, he or she stands up. If the student believes the statement is false, he or she remains seated. The teacher calls on two or three students who hold differing views (either standing or sitting). Each is then asked to explain his or her rationale for standing or sitting. After a student provides a reason for his or her answer, the other students may change their minds and either join the group who are standing or join the others who are sitting. The students' explanations help others to rethink which is the most reasonable or correct/incorrect answer to the question. As this happens, the teacher can take advantage of the teachable moment. Stand Up–Sit Down is a quick assessment of comprehension during lesson delivery, while at the same time students can clarify their own understanding. Older students can create their own true/false statements related to a subject area, and "test" their peers' reactions to the statements.

SIOP Connection

Content Objective

Students will be able to determine if statements made about (a topic) are true or false, and provide a rationale for their decisions.

Language Objective

Students will be able to state their explanation for why they believe a statement about (a topic) is true or false by using the following sentence frames:

"I believe that statement is true, because _____."

"I believe that statement is false, because _____."

Heading Into Questions

(Adapted from Angie Medina, Long Beach Unified School District)

- ■ **Grade Levels:** 1–12
- ■ **Subject Areas:** All
- ■ **Grouping Configurations:** Individual, partners, small groups, or whole class
- ■ **Approximate Time Involved:** 5–30 minutes (depending on grouping configuration)

Description

The objective of Heading Into Questions is to give students a purpose for reading. As a teacher delivers a lesson, it is crucial to keep in mind that students need a purpose so that they may see the path they are to follow while reading. The students look at the bold headings in the reading to predict the types of questions that may be asked in reference to the information in the text. Initially the activity should be done with the whole class, so that the students may have the strategy properly modeled. Using the text copied on transparencies, the teacher models how to turn the headings of a chapter into questions by adding questioning words (*who, what, where, when, why, how*). These questions become the focus and purpose of the reading. Students use the questions to monitor their comprehension throughout that section of the text. After they receive frequent opportunities for guided practice, students can create Heading Into Questions individually, in partners, or in small groups. No matter how students are grouped, they can split up the task, turn each heading into a question, write the questions, and then present the questions to the class. The questions can be written on chart paper and the answers filled in during the lesson delivery.

SIOP Connection

Content Objective

Students will be able to turn chapter headings into key questions and then answer these questions after reading about (a topic).

Language Objective

Students will be able to use question words (*who, what, where, when, why, how*) to turn headings into questions.

Chunk and Chew

(Adapted from Jo Gusman, New Horizons in Education, Inc.)

- **Grade Levels:** All
- **Subject Areas:** All
- **Grouping Configurations:** Individual, partners, small groups, or whole class
- **Approximate Time Involved:** Duration of lesson

Description

The purpose of Chunk and Chew is to ensure that students are not inundated with input from the teacher without being given appropriate time to process the information. By following the Chunk and Chew strategy, teachers deliver their lessons is small "chunks" and then give students time to "chew" the information either individually, with partners, or in small groups. Teachers should follow this simple rule: for every 10 minutes of teacher input, students should be given 2 minutes to process the information. (This is known as 10 and 2.) Time frames from input and processing vary and should be adjusted according to language proficiency and grade level. When students are aware of the Chunk and Chew strategy, they anticipate the processing time and let the teacher know when they have reached their limit on input.

SIOP Connection

This particular activity for Lesson Delivery does not lend itself to specific content or language objectives, as it is information for the teacher to use when teaching a lesson.

Magic Buttons

(Adapted from Angie Medina, Long Beach Unified School District)

- ■ **Grade Levels:** K–4

- ■ **Subject Areas:** All

- ■ **Grouping Configurations:** Individuals or partners

- ■ **Approximate Time Involved:** 1 minute

Description

The purpose of Magic Buttons is to allow students think-time during a lesson. Every student is given two buttons: an "I'm thinking!" button and an "I got it!" button. After the teacher poses a question, the students' hands should remain on the "I'm thinking" button until they have had sufficient time to process the information. When they are ready to respond, students should move to the "I got it!" button to show that their thinking is complete. This strategy allows the teacher to monitor the students' think-time to ensure that adequate time is given to process the information. This strategy shows students the importance of the thinking process, rather than simply validating the correct answer. Once the majority of class members have their hands on the "I got it!" button the teacher can than move the discussion to partners, small groups, or whole class. Another version of Magic Buttons is to give students an opportunity to agree or disagree non-verbally through pressing a button.

SIOP Connection

Content Objective

Students will be able to monitor their own thinking and processing by deciding (after think-time) when they are ready to respond to a teacher's questions.

Language Objective

Students will be able to orally explain their responses and how they decided on them after they are given sufficient think-time.

Magic Buttons

Magic Buttons

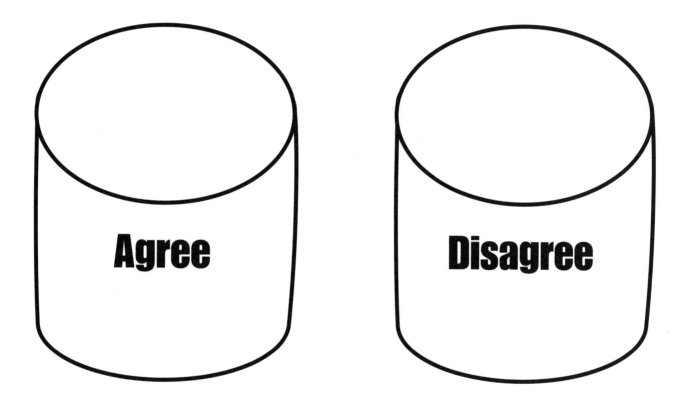

Procedural Knowledge

(Adapted from Lipson & Wixson, 2003)

- ■ **Grade Levels:** All
- ■ **Subject Areas:** All
- ■ **Grouping Configuration:** Whole class
- ■ **Approximate Time Involved:** 15–20 minutes

Description

The purpose of Procedural Knowledge is to allow students to become familiar with the procedural steps of a particular learning or instructional strategy. Remember that learning strategies are those acquired behaviors (such as routinely predicting and previewing) that learners use to make sense of new information; they "reside" in the learner's head. Instructional strategies are those techniques, methods, and approaches teachers use to help students acquire necessary learning behaviors (such as SQP2RS and most of the ideas presented in this Handbook).

When introducing a new learning or instructional strategy during lesson delivery, it is important to remember that students need time to understand the procedural steps before they attempt to connect the strategy to content. The first time students use a strategy, it is helpful if the topic is something that is very familiar to the students (e.g., favorite foods or hobbies). This ensures that the procedures will be learned and students will not be sidetracked by unfamiliar content. Once students understand the procedure, they can use the strategy in connection with content. When a learning or instructional strategy is frequently reinforced, the procedure becomes secondary and students begin to tackle the content with ease. It is best to implement one strategy at a time so that the students become familiar with the procedure. Repeating the same strategy helps students "own" it so that they can use it again and again with very little teacher instruction.

Marge Lipson and Karen Wixson (2003) also suggest that teachers emphasize Declarative Knowledge (what the strategy is) and Conditional Knowledge (under what conditions or circumstances one might need to employ the strategy). If students just follow the procedural steps without understanding what kind of strategic thinking they're using, the chance of their internalizing the strategy is minimal at best.

SIOP Connection

This particular activity for Lesson Delivery does not lend itself to specific content or language objectives, as it is information for the teacher to use when planning the delivery of a lesson.

Response Cards

- ■ **Grade Levels:** All

- ■ **Subject Areas:** All

- ■ **Grouping Configurations:** Individual, partners, small groups

- ■ **Approximate Time Involved:** 5 minutes

Description

The purpose of Response Cards is to allow students to respond non-verbally to questions that have an answer of 1–4 or a–d. Each student is given a sheet of paper with the numbers 1–4 on one side and the letters a–d on the other. The students fold the paper in fourths so that only one number or letter is showing at a time. The teacher reads a question either from the overhead, chart, text, or test practice book, then reads the four possible choices. The students respond by folding the Response Card to show the number or letter that corresponds with the answer they believe to be true. As the students become more efficient in the implementation of the strategy, they read the questions and the possible answer choices. This strategy can be modified by giving one Response Card to each small group or set of partners.

Response Cards can also be made with 2" × 6" strips of tagboard. On one side of the card, write (vertically) the numbers 0, 1, 2, 3, 4. The zero indicates "I don't know" or "I'm not sure." In response to a question with multiple choice possibilities, students place their index fingers on the pertinent number. These Response Cards can fulfill two purposes if "Agree" and "Disagree" are written at the top and bottom of the other side of the card. When students are asked a question about which they can agree or disagree, they hold up the appropriate response. The most beneficial aspect of Response Cards is that they provide the teacher with immediate feedback about how well students comprehend the lesson content.

For standardized test preparation, numbers can be replaced by the letters a, b, c, d.

SIOP Connection

This particular activity for Lesson Delivery does not lend itself to specific content or language objectives, as it is information for the teacher to use when planning the delivery of a lesson.

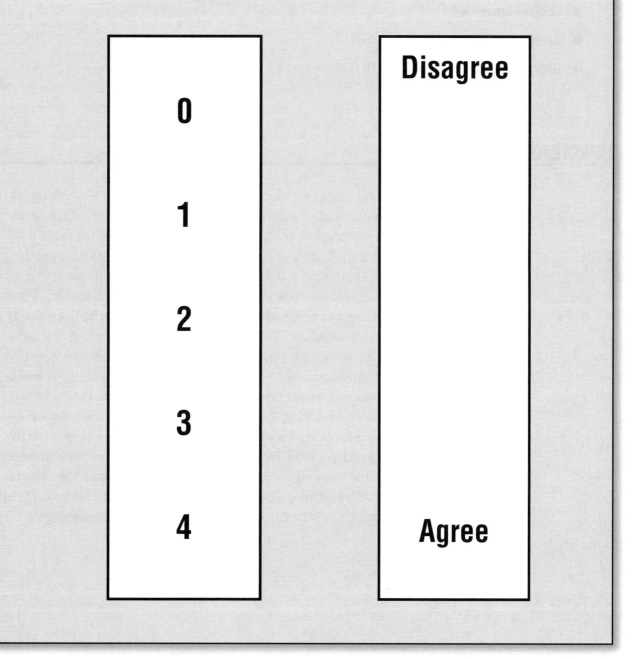

0

1

2

3

4

Disagree

Agree

Secret Answer

(Adapted from Angie Medina, Long Beach Unified School District)

- ■ **Grade Levels:** K–8
- ■ **Subject Areas:** All
- ■ **Grouping Configuration:** Individual
- ■ **Approximate Time Involved:** 1–15 minutes

Description

During Secret Answer, students respond with a hand signal close to their chest to show their answer to a particular question. As a question is posed either orally by the teacher or from reading in a text, the students are given options for the answer that are labeled as 1, 2, 3, or 4. As students listen to the question and think about the answer, they make a fist. When the teacher cues them, students show the number of fingers they think corresponds to the correct answer. The strategy is titled Secret Answer to emphasize that the answer to the question is between each individual student and the teacher. Rather than holding the number answer up high in the air, which takes away individual accountability and minimizes think-time, signaling Secret Answers encourages students to answer independently and allows them to process at their own pace. The teacher can monitor comprehension by checking the Secret Answers, validating correct answers, and encouraging rethinking for incorrect responses. This is a great activity for supporting test practice, because it allows students to have their answers to test questions validated immediately. Secret Answer also enables the teacher to monitor comprehension and keeps each student engaged with the task. Older students may prefer to use the Response Cards to accomplish the same goal.

SIOP Connection

This particular activity for Lesson Delivery does not lend itself to specific content or language objectives, as it is information for the teacher to use when planning the delivery of a lesson.

Take Your Corners

(Adapted from Kagan, 1994)

- ■ **Grade Levels:** 2–12
- ■ **Subject Areas:** All
- ■ **Grouping Configuration:** Whole class
- ■ **Approximate Time Involved:** 20–40 minutes

Description

Take Your Corners allows students to show their opinion through physical movement in a nonthreatening way. Each corner of the room is labeled with a particular category or opinion. The students do a quick-draw on an index card to represent their opinion. The students mix around the room sharing their quick-draw with others until the teacher calls "Freeze." At this point the students are encouraged to point to the corner related to their opinion. When the teacher calls, "Go," students walk to their respective corners and share their opinions with one another. The teacher can roam from corner to corner to monitor understanding and take advantage of any teachable moments. As the students are separated into their corners, the instruction can become whole class as all students look to the teacher for clarification or debate their opinions against students in the other corners. This activity works well at the beginning of instruction, during the lesson delivery, and as closure to a lesson.

SIOP Connection

Content Objective

Students will be able to choose one of four opinions (e.g., one of four presidents who they feel made the most meaningful contributions to American society) and defend their opinions based on the information they have acquired through instruction and research.

Language Objectives

- Students will be able to state their opinions while showing respect for others' opinions by using the following sentence frames:

  "I believe _____."

  "I feel _____."

  "My opinion is _____."

- Students will be able to disagree with other students while showing respect for others' opinions by using the following sentence frames:

  "I disagree with that statement about _____, because _____."

  "I can understand your opinion, but _____."

  "Have you ever thought of _____?"

What Do You Know?

■ **Grade Levels:** K–12

■ **Subject Areas:** All

■ **Grouping Configuration:** Small groups or whole class

■ **Approximate Time Involved:** 5–15 minutes (depending on group discussion)

Description

Often students are verbally questioned about what they know about a particular topic, so that a teacher may assess their understanding. When English learners are asked the question, "What do you know about _____?" the answer may be limited or even a blank stare. A student's inability to answer may not indicate a total lack of comprehension, but rather a lack of connection to the topic. When a teacher poses a question while at the same time showing photos, illustrations, and/or realia, the student then has something with which to connect. This small bit of support allows for a more accurate assessment of understanding and it facilitates more efficient comprehension. Teachers may obtain photos or illustrations from textbooks or other resources and copy the photos or illustrations on a transparency or enlarge them for the whole class to view. Realia, which consist of artifacts and real-life materials related to the content, can be obtained by the teacher through school resources or by the students through items they may have at home. When English learners see something at the same time they hear about it, their chances for understanding the topic are enhanced.

SIOP Connection

This particular activity for Lesson Delivery does not lend itself to specific content or language objectives, as it is information for the teacher to use when planning the delivery of a lesson.

Stop That Video

(Adapted from Long Beach Unified School District)

- ■ **Grade Levels:** All
- ■ **Subject Areas:** All
- ■ **Grouping Configuration:** Whole class
- ■ **Approximate Time Involved:** 30–60 minutes (depending on grade level and the length of the video)

Description

English learners (and others) watching a content-related video may attempt to talk during the course of the video, be asked to quiet down, and when finished viewing the video have nothing to share related to the content. This problem may be due to inadequate processing time, and it can be resolved by using the Stop That Video technique.

During this activity, the teacher stops the video at key points and allows the students time to process the information individually, either in their heads or on paper. English learners particularly benefit from note-taking sheets that outline key points or questions to be answered in the video. Once students process information independently, they can share and clarify the information with a partner.

This strategy allows the teacher to check for understanding throughout the course of the video and address any misconceptions. If a student chooses to process the information with another student in their primary language, their comprehension will most likely be enhanced.

SIOP Connection

Content Objective

While viewing a video on (a topic), students will be able to stop periodically and summarize what they have just seen.

Language Objective

Students will be able to use sequence words (e.g., *in the beginning, then, next, before, after, finally,* etc.) to summarize what they have seen in a video on (a topic).

▪ SIOP Features ▪

27. Comprehensive review of key vocabulary

28. Comprehensive review of key content concepts

29. Regular feedback provided to students on their output (e.g., language, content, work)

30. Assessment of student comprehension and learning of all lesson objectives (e.g., spot checking, group response) throughout the lesson

Share Bear

(Adapted from Angie Medina, Long Beach Unified School District)

- ■ **Grade Levels:** K–3
- ■ **Subject Areas:** All
- ■ **Grouping Configuration:** Small groups
- ■ **Approximate Time Involved:** 5–10 minutes for the discussion (depending on the teacher's purposes)

Description

The purpose of Share Bear is to encourage all students in a table group to engage in higher-level thinking, participate, and wait their turn. Each table has one Share Bear (a stuffed animal). After the teacher poses an open ended question (e.g., "How did you feel when?" "Why did the _____?" "What do you remember about _____?" "How would you _____?") one student at each table is instructed to take the Share Bear. That student gives his or her response to the question then passes the Share Bear to the next student who then gives his or her response. This continues until each student has had multiple turns or until each student has shared. The teacher walks around the room and if he or she hears language errors (e.g., "The boy *go,* because . . ."), the teacher may interject (e.g., "Right, the boy *went* because . . .").

SIOP Connection

Content Objective

Students will be able to take turns answering questions, discussing, and explaining information about (a topic).

Language Objective

Students will be able to use following sentence frames:

"I think that _____."

"I believe that _____ because _____."

Simultaneous Roundtable

(Adapted from Kagan, 1994)

- **Grade Levels:** All

- **Subject Areas:** All

- **Grouping Configuration:** Small groups

- **Approximate Time Involved:** 10 minutes

Description

The purpose of Simultaneous Roundtable is for students to help each other as they review. Each student at the table group (four or five students) is given a paper and a pencil. The students label the papers with their team number, rather than their own names, because the paper will be passed around the group. The teacher poses a question with multiple short answers. Students are given a short time period (two minutes) to respond to the question and are then told to pass the papers to each group member four or five times. Each time the paper is passed to a student, he or she must read what is already on the list and then add his or her ideas. The student may write an answer that he or she may have seen on another piece of paper or create a new answer. This strategy allows students to review individually, yet with the support of their team members.

For example, through the activity of Simultaneous Roundtable, students could review what they learned about pioneers through reading their peers' writing and then adding their own ideas. The lists circulate around the table until complete, and when the activity comes to an end, each student reads his or her list to their team. The teacher can generate one class list of information about pioneers when the teams report.

SIOP Connection

Content Objective

Students will be able to generate a list of answers about (a topic).

Language Objectives

▶ Students will be able to write their ideas about key information on the list.

▶ Students will be able to read and discuss listed ideas.

Find Someone Who

(Adapted from Kagan, 1994)

- ■ **Grade Levels:** 2–12
- ■ **Subject Areas:** All
- ■ **Grouping Configuration:** Whole class
- ■ **Approximate Time Involved:** 10–15 minutes

Description

The purpose of Find Someone Who is to have the students help each other review previously taught information. Students are given a review sheet and they circulate around the room to find help in answering the questions on the sheet. They approach one another and ask a question. If a student knows the answer, he tells it and the other student writes it on his own review sheet. The student who gave the information signs or initials next to the answer. Each student may give information to no more than one question on another student's paper. After a given time, students take their seats and the teacher facilitates a review of the answers so that students can check their papers for accuracy.

SIOP Connection

Content Objectives

▶ Students will be able to ask and answer questions about (a topic).

▶ Students will be able to decide if other students' answers are correct or incorrect.

Language Objectives

▶ Students will be able to read questions to other students.

▶ Students will be able to listen to another student's answer to a question and then write that response, if it is deemed correct, on the review sheet.

▶ Students will be able to orally tell a correct answer to a question posed by another student.

Numbered Heads Together With a Review Sheet

(Adapted from Kagan, 1994)

- ■ **Grade Levels:** 3–12
- ■ **Subject Areas:** All
- ■ **Grouping Configuration:** Small groups
- ■ **Approximate Time Involved:** 5 minutes

Description

The purpose of Numbered Heads Together With a Review Sheet is to offer peer support for review of unit content. Each student is given a review sheet and a pencil. The teacher reads the first question aloud to the students. Students put their heads together in each group to reach consensus on the answer. They can use the text or other resources to determine their group answer (e.g., instruments for a unit on measurement). The teacher then calls a number and students from each table with that number stand to answer for the small groups. If a student's answer is incorrect, the teacher may respond, "I can see how your team might think that, but actually the answer is _____." Once the correct answer is determined, the students write the answer on their review sheet. The process is continued with all of the questions on the review sheet. Students review, using listening, speaking, reading, and writing, and they are able to do so with group interaction and support.

SIOP Connection

Content Objective

Students will be able to work in a group to review information about (a topic).

Language Objective

Students will be able to listen to questions, generate answers in writing, and orally report the answers to class members.

Sign In, Please

- **Grade Levels:** All
- **Subject Areas:** All
- **Grouping Configuration:** Individual
- **Approximate Time Involved:** 5 minutes (depending on the teacher)

Description

The purpose of Sign In, Please, is to assess students' understanding of the content of a lesson. This instructional strategy can be used throughout the lesson. The sign for T (true) is a fist with the thumb protruding between the index and middle finger. The sign for F (false) is the middle, ring, and little finger extended with the thumb holding the fingernail of the index finger flat to the palm. Throughout the lesson the teacher makes a statement and asks if the statement is true or false. Students respond with hand signs for true or false. When the teacher sees students with the incorrect response, she explains why the statement is true or false or asks students to explain their rationale.

SIOP Connection

Content Objective

Students will be able to determine whether a statement is true or false and indicate a response using sign language.

Language Objective

Students will be able to listen carefully to statements before determining if they are true or false.

Response Boards

- ■ **Grade Level:** 1–12
- ■ **Subject Areas:** All
- ■ **Grouping Configurations:** Individual, partners, or small groups
- ■ **Approximate Time Involved:** 5–10 minutes

Description

The purpose of Response Boards is to give the teacher a chance to assess whether students have grasped the fundamentals of a lesson before moving on. Each student, each pair, or each group is given a response board. The teacher poses a problem or a question for the students to answer. If the students are working in pairs or small groups, a designated student writes and displays the response board after conferencing with the partner or group. The teacher can see if the class is ready to progress beyond that point.

There are a variety of ways to create response boards: laminated file folders or tag board (used with vis-à-vis markers or crayon), white boards (inexpensively made with tile board, available at home improvement/lumber stores), chalkboards, or paper and pencil. A response board might also include graphics or illustrations related to the content that the students may point to for their response.

SIOP Connection

This particular activity for Review and Assessment does not lend itself to specific content or language objectives, as it is information for the teacher to use when planning the review of a lesson.

Find the Fib

(Adapted from Kagan, 1994)

- **Grade Levels:** All

- **Subject Areas:** All

- **Grouping Configurations:** Individual, partners, small groups

- **Approximate Time Involved:** 10 minutes if the teacher makes the statements; 15 minutes for the students to write the statements and as much time as the teacher feels necessary to find the fibs

Description

The purpose of Find the Fib is for the teacher to assess the students' understanding of facts while they are supported in their decision making by peers. The students each have a set of three cards that say: #1 is the fib, #2 is the fib, #3 is the fib. If students are working in pairs or small groups they may each have a set of cards or they may share a set of cards. The teacher poses a set of statements: one is false and the other two are true. The students may also write their own statements (one false and two true). The students then decide independently, with their partner, or in their small groups which one is false (the fib). On a signal from the teacher, students show their cards. If a student has the wrong answer, the teacher asks other students to explain which word in the fib makes it false. The teacher can also encourage the class to explain which word or phrase in the true statements makes them true.

SIOP Connection

Content Objective

Students will be able to determine whether statements about (a topic) are true or false.

Language Objectives

▶ Students will be able to listen to statements about (a topic) orally presented by the teacher.

▶ Students will be able to discuss with group members true and false statements about (a topic).

▶ Students will be able to write true and false statements about (a topic).

Selected References

Asher, J. J. (1982). The total physical response approach. In R. W. Blair (Ed.). *Innovative approaches to language teaching* (pp. 54–66). Rowley, MA: Newbury House.

Bear, D., Templeton, S., Invernizzi, M., & Johnston, F. (2004). *Words their way: Word study for phonics, vocabulary, and spelling* (3rd ed.). Upper Saddle River, NJ: Merrill/ Prentice-Hall.

Echevarria, J., Vogt, M. E., & Short, D. J. (2004). *Making content comprehensible for English learners: The SIOP model* (2nd ed.). Boston: Allyn & Bacon.

Holbrook, S. (2005). *Practical poetry: A nonstandard approach to meeting content-area standards.* Portsmouth, NJ: Heinemann.

Jackson, S. (1982). *The lottery: And other stories.* New York: Farrar, Straus and Giroux.

Kagan, S. (1994). *Cooperative learning.* San Clemente, CA: Kagan.

Lipson, M., & Wixson, K. (2003). *Assessment and instruction of reading and writing difficulty: An interactive approach* (3rd ed.). Boston: Allyn & Bacon.

Macon, J., Buell, D., & Vogt, M. E. (1991). *Responses to literature: Grades K–8.* Newark, DE: International Reading Association.

Ogle, D. (1986). K-W-L: A teaching model that develops active reading of expository text. *The Reading Teacher, 39*(6), 564–570.

Raphael, T. E. (1984). Teaching learners about sources of information for answering comprehension questions. *Journal of Reading, 27*(4), 303–311.

Readence, J. E., Bean, T. W., & Baldwin, R. S. (2001). *Content area literacy: An integrated approach* (7th ed.). Dubuque, IA: Kendall/Hunt Publishing Company.

Say, A. (1993). *Grandfather's journey.* Boston: Houghton Mifflin Company.

Schultz, A. (1998). *Creative reading activities.* (Workshop Handout). Long Beach, CA: Beach Cities Reading Association.

Stauffer, R. (1969). *Teaching reading as a thinking process.* New York: Harper & Row.

Temple, C. (1998). *Reading and Writing for Critical Thinking Project.* (Workshop Handout). International Reading Association.

Vogt, M. E. (2000). Active learning in the content areas. In M. McLaughlin & M. E. Vogt (Eds.), *Creativity and innovation in content area teaching.* Norwood, MA: Christopher-Gordon Publishers.